The Kids'

CODE
and
CIPHER
BOOK

The Kids'
CODE
and
CIPHER
BOOK

NANCY GARDEN

Holt, Rinehart and Winston / New York

Library of Congress Cataloging in Publication Data

Garden, Nancy.   The kids' code and cipher book.
Summary: Presents a variety of codes and
ciphers and includes messages to encode and decode,
nearly all of which are part of a story.
1. Ciphers—Juvenile literature. [1. Ciphers]
I. Title.   Z103.3.G35   652'.8   80-10434
ISBN hc: 0-03-053856-4
ISBN pb: 0-03-059267-4

To Sue, Sam, Scott, and Rob
with love

Contents

Introduction

What do twisted paths and dancing men have in common with a rail fence?

My seventh-grade science teacher, who loved questions like that, would probably have said something like "They all take up space," or "They're all made up of atoms." She'd be right, of course—except in this case she'd be wrong.

Twisted Paths, Dancing Men, and Rail Fence are the names of three different ciphers.

A cipher is a kind of secret writing. So is a code. You'll be reading about both in this book. People usually use ciphers to disguise single letters, and codes to disguise words or phrases.

Ciphers and codes have been used for centuries for sending secret messages. In wartime, spies, diplomats, and armies use complicated machines to ENcipher and ENcode (put messages *into* cipher and code) and to DEcipher and DEcode (take them out again). But ciphers and codes are also used in peacetime, usually as nonsecret shortcuts. Computer programmers use nonsecret codes to make facts and figures simple enough to be stored in a machine's "memory." Businesses save money by using codes to shorten telegrams and cablegrams. Stores and manufacturers use codes that seem secret (those funny-looking lines on cereal boxes, for instance). But most of those codes are really just ways of writing prices, expiration dates, and other information so they can be "read" by machines.

You yourself may know people who use ciphers or codes. Have you ever heard someone say "10-4"? That means "Okay" or "Message received" in a code originally used by long-distance truck drivers. Maybe your family has special code words or phrases for things you don't want outsiders to overhear. "FHB" and "MIK" are used in my family in front of company, to mean "Family hold back" when there isn't enough of some kind of food, and "More in kitchen" when there is. Maybe you have a secret code that you use with a friend—or perhaps you've experimented with Morse or semaphore.

There are hundreds of codes and ciphers and hundreds of ways to use them—ways that range from saving lives to having fun. This book will show you some of the most useful codes and ciphers, and some of the oldest. It will also show you how to make up a few of your own, and how to make and use code and cipher "machines." Along the way, you'll find lots of secret messages to solve, many of which are part of a story that runs through most of the book. (The answers are given at the end of each chapter.)

In the last chapter, for those of you who are especially interested, there are some general rules for cracking secret messages. And—for everyone—there are more messages to solve. At the very end there's a list of other books you might want to read and a glossary of code and cipher terms.

You'll need a few things to work on the codes and ciphers in this book. The main ones are paper (lined is better than unlined), plus tracing or other see-through paper, and a good batch of sharp pencils, with erasers. You can manage very well with those until you get to the chapter on code and cipher machines. For that chapter, you'll need scissors, tape, glue, lightweight cardboard, cardboard cylinders, a pen, and a ruler. You don't absolutely need graph paper, but it will be a tremendous help throughout the book if you can get some. About five little squares to the inch is a good size. You may find a few colored pencils useful too.

Good luck and have fun!

Nancy Garden
Carlisle, Massachusetts

1 | Scrambled Alphabets

Since the *Mary Ann*'s captain is an expert in cipher, it
probably won't take him very long to decipher these messages—take them out of cipher. But he also probably spent

years becoming an expert—which is another way of saying that it's okay for you to take all the time you need to decipher any message, especially at first.

Look again at the message the stranger handed Captain Snow:

REGNAD SETARIP RAEN TSAOC

And look at the second message, the one the stranger handed the first mate:

TSAOC RAENS ETARI PREGN ADXYZ

Notice anything? Do you see that the *last* word in the *first* message is the same as the *first* word in the second message? Could that mean that the second message is the first message—*backwards*?

That's close but not quite true. Something's backwards, though! Here's another clue: The *first* message is in what some people call Backwards Word Cipher and the *second* is in Backwards Message Cipher.

(Don't feel bad about getting clues so early. One of the most important things to remember about ciphers is that they're almost impossible to DEcipher unless you have some idea of how they were ENciphered. The same thing goes for codes. That's why professional spies have code books, cipher machines, and other helpful tools. Only a real expert can look at a strange cipher and figure it out without any clues. Even so, it often takes experts days or even weeks of hard work—and once in a while they end up stumped anyway!)

Okay. Keeping in mind the name *Backwards* <u>*Word*</u> *Cipher*, take another look at message number 1:

REGNAD SETARIP RAEN TSAOC

On a piece of lined paper write:

REGNAD

By now you've probably already thought of trying REG-NAD backwards:

REGNAD—DANGER

And, as you can see, that idea works! That's exactly how this cipher was written. In Backwards Word Cipher, then, *each word* of the real message is written down backwards.

Try the next word in the first message: SETARIP. Backwards, it spells:

SETARIP—PIR _ _ _ _ ?

And now try the other two words. (It's a good idea, by the way, to write your DEciphered message right above the ENciphered one.)

_ _ _ _   _ _ _ _ _ ?

R A E N   T S A O C

The answer is Number 1 on page 10, but you may not even need to look it up. If you don't, congratulations! You just cracked your first cipher!

That cipher—and also the one Captain Snow's mate got, which we'll work on in a minute—is an example of what is called *transposition* cipher. You put a message into a transposition cipher by rearranging its letters. Copying the letters down in backwards order is just one of many ways to rearrange them. Actually, you can make up a transposition cipher by scrambling the letters any old way—without any plan or pattern. But keep in mind that it's extra hard to solve a cipher if you don't know how it's been written. If you're exchanging secret messages with a friend, decide together ahead of time just how you'll scramble the letters.

Let's go back to the Backwards Word Cipher for a minute. You already know how to DEcipher a message written in that cipher: Just write each ENciphered word down backwards. REGNAD becomes DANGER, SETARIP becomes PIRATES, and so on. To put a message *into* Backwards Word Cipher—to ENcipher it—all you have to do is write out your real message and then write each word down again backwards. The real word BACKWARDS, then, is enciphered:

BACKWARDS

SDRAW _ _ _ _ ?

(The answer is Number 2 on page 10.)

Here are a couple more Backwards Word Cipher messages for practice:

3. DEcipher:

OHW SI ETARIP NIATPAC

4. ENcipher:

ST CYR IS PIRATE CAPTAIN

(The answers are on pages 10 and 11.)

The name of the cipher used for the second message—the one the stranger handed Captain Snow's first mate—should give you a clue as to how it works: *Backwards Message Cipher*, another kind of transposition.

Here's that message again:

TSAOC RAENS ETARI PREGN ADXYZ

Write that down on the second line of a clean sheet of paper. Then above it, on the top line, write it backwards, letter by letter, starting with the Z. Keep the "words" the same length:

ZYXDA NGERP IRATE SNEAR COAST
TSAOC RAENS ETARI PREGN ADXYZ

At first glance, that doesn't look like much. But take a closer look at the top line. Look at the last word, COAST. And the next to last word: if you drop the S from the beginning of it, you have NEAR. The third word, IRATE, is a real word as is, but it doesn't make much sense in the message (which at this point looks suspiciously like the message Snow himself was handed). But if you take the P from the end of the second word, NGERP, and the S from the beginning of SNEAR, and stick them onto opposite ends of IRATE, you get PIRATES! That leaves you with ZYXDA NGER. (There's no P at the end of that anymore because you used the P in PIRATES.) If you take the DA from ZYXDA and add it to what you have left of NGER, you get—DANGER!

Look at the whole message this way:

ZYXDA NGERP IRATE SNEAR COAST
or
ZYX DANGER PIRATES NEAR COAST

The stranger did three things to put this message into Backwards Message Cipher. (The last step will tell you about the ZYX and XYZ.)

1. He wrote the *real* message down backwards—the whole thing, letter by letter:

TSAOC RAEN SETARIP REGNAD

He could have left it like that, but in order to make it harder to decipher, he also:

2. Divided the now-enciphered message into fake five-letter "words":

TSAOC RAENS ETARI PREGN AD
and

3. Because the last "word" had only two letters in it, he made it match the others by adding *nulls*. Nulls are extra letters that have nothing to do with either the message or the cipher:

TSAOC RAENS ETARI PREGN AD<u>XYZ</u>
nulls

And there you have the complete message!

Let's look at those last two steps more closely. They are important tricks of the cipher trade, and you'll be using them often in this book. The reason for Step 2 is that it's much too easy to decipher a word if it stays its real length. So:

■ Make your cipher messages hard to decipher by dividing them into fake "words." (Most people make each "word" five letters long.) Put your message into cipher first, and then just divide the words into groups of five letters each.

A lot of messages won't have the right number of letters to divide evenly into five-letter "words"; the last "word" will sometimes have only four letters, or three, two, or one. That's the reason for Step 3:

■ To confuse your enemy even more, fill in any empty space or spaces in an enciphered message with nulls.

You do have to be a little careful with nulls, though. In Backwards Message Cipher, for example, you can use any letters you want for nulls—*except* letters that spell something backwards. TAC, for instance, wouldn't work well as nulls at the end of the mate's message. What would the message read deciphered, with those letters for nulls?

TSAOC RAENS ETARI PREGN ADTAC

(The answer is Number 5 on page 11.)

It wouldn't make much difference, though, if the nulls were DAB, even though those letters do spell something backwards:

TSAOC RAENS ETARI PREGN ADDAB

(This message is deciphered in Number 6 on page 11.)

In fact, those nulls work so well that you could even make them an official part of the real message!

But what about these for nulls?

TSAOC RAENS ETARI PREGN ADONX

(Message deciphered in Number 7 on page 11.)

You'll be using nulls a lot as you go along in this book. They're very handy and, used right, they can help confuse anyone who tries to break (solve) your cipher.

Remember:

To ENcipher a message in Backwards Message Cipher:

1. Write the real message down backwards. Since you'll be putting it into five-letter "words" anyway, you can

write it out in one long line if you want, with no spaces between the original words. (The real word lengths were kept the first time to show you more clearly about dividing into fake words.)

2. Divide the backwards message into five-letter "words."

3. Add nulls to the last "word" if it turns out to be fewer than five letters long.

To DEcipher a message in Backwards Message Cipher, you really do very much the same thing as you did to ENcipher it.

Let's say you've received the message:

LIASN IAMEH TTSIO HQXYZ

Since each "word" in the message is five letters long, you can be almost certain the message has been divided into fake words. You might as well ignore the word divisions. Therefore, your first step in deciphering is:

1. Write the whole message down *backwards* in one long line without word divisions. (Remember that the real message was written down backwards when it was ENciphered. When you write the enciphered message down backwards, then, you're really just turning it around so it's frontwards again.)

2. Cross out any obvious nulls—letters at the beginning that don't spell anything. (The nulls are now at the beginning because you've turned the message around.)

3. Read along the message carefully till you find the first possible word, and then copy that word down:

~~ZYXQ~~HOISTTHEMAINSAIL

HOIST

4. Keep doing that till you have a message that makes sense.

Doing this is a little like playing those find-the-word games where you have to pick out all the words hidden in a large block of letters. It may take a little time, and you may find that you make a few false starts. For example, the second word in the above message could be:

~~ZYXQ~~HOIST**THEM**AINSAIL
or
~~ZYXQ~~HOIST**THE**MAINSAIL

You should be able to tell which version is right if you go a little further. If, for example, you decide the second word in this message is THEM, you'll have a hard time finding other words that make sense:

HOIST THEM AINSAIL ?
HOIST THEM A IN SAIL ?
HOIST THEM A I NSAIL ?

Only the word THE really works:

HOIST THE MAINSAIL

Here are a couple of messages in Backwards Message Cipher for you to practice with:

8. DEcipher:

SETAR IPFON GISON

9. ENcipher:

SEND THE LOOKOUT ALOFT

(Remember to divide the enciphered message into five-letter "words" and to add nulls if you need them.)

(The answers are on page 11.)

Remember that in *transposition ciphers* you always have all the letters of the real message right in front of you. All you have to do is sort them out. Sometimes that's as easy as turning a backwards message right side around. But sometimes—as you'll see in the next chapter—it's not quite as simple as that. There are many more clever ways to scramble the letters of a secret message!

Answers for Chapter One

1. DANGER PIRATES NEAR COAST

REGNAD SETARIP RAEN TSAOC

2. BACKWARDS

SDRAWKCAB

3. WHO   IS   PIRATE   CAPTAIN

OHW   SI   ETARIP   NIATPAC

4. ST CYR IS PIRATE CAPTAIN
   TS RYC SI ETARIP NIATPAC

5. CAT DANGER PIRATES NEAR COAST

6. BAD DANGER PIRATES NEAR COAST

7. X still works as a null here. But O and N do not—
   because deciphered, the message would read:
       (X) NO DANGER PIRATES NEAR COAST
   —which is exactly the opposite of what the message is
   trying to say!

8. NO SIGN OF PIRATES
   SETAR IPFON GISON

9. SEND THE LOOKOUT ALOFT
   TFOLA TUOKO OLEHT DNES<u>X</u>
   (Nulls in answers will be underlined from now on.)

2 | More Scrambled Alphabets

From the secret diary of Samuel Snow, son of Captain Joshua Snow and now a prisoner aboard the pirate schooner Barbary Scourge

Sept. 4

Today my captors let me walk awhile on deck but I am still weak and sick from the wounds I received at their hands two months ago. It looks as if my guess was right that we are now off the Carolinas. I hope my warning reached my father, but I know it was a risk to trust it to an ex-pirate, no matter how much he wants revenge for his treatment at the cruel hands of this cruel captain, St. Cyr of the *Barbary Scourge,* who rules this ship like an ancient tyrant. Oh, to see the *Mary Ann* come into view on the horizon—but no, I must not wish it, for surely the pirates would board her to steal her cargo and take my father prisoner with all his crew. Father must not come upon this devil ship till he is duly warned—and to my joy I have now found here in the bilge where they keep me the means of warning him further. I have discovered a store of empty bottles from the pirates' nightly revels and so I will soon enclose this message—THE SCHOONER FLIES FALSE COLORS—in several bottles and throw them over the side to warn my father and any other honest seamen who ply these waters. I shall disguise the message, I think, in Rail

Fence Cipher, for that is quick and Father knows it well.
. . . But soft! Someone comes! I must quickly replace this
little book under the friendly plank that hides it and close
my eyes in pretended sleep.

Rail Fence Cipher is indeed quick—and fun to do.

1. Copy the real message down on a clean sheet of
paper:

THE SCHOONER FLIES FALSE COLORS

(By now you've probably noticed that the messages
have all been written in capital letters. It's safer that way.
If you use both capital and small letters, you'll risk giving
clues to your enemies about things like which word comes
first and which letters are parts of proper names.)

2. Count the number of letters in the message. If it
doesn't come out to an even number, add a null to the end.
There are 27 letters in this message. Add a null to make
it 28.

THE SCHOONER FLIES FALSE COLORS X

3. Now write the message down again, this time in two
staggered rows, with a space after each letter. (It's easier
to use lined paper or graph paper for this. If you use graph
paper, it should have squares large enough for you to write
in comfortably. If there are more than five squares per
inch, the squares are probably too small!) The first letter of
the message goes in the *top* row. The second letter goes in
the *bottom* row, a little to the right of the first letter. Then
the third letter goes in the *top* row, a little to the right of
the second letter- like this:

T E C O N R L E F L E O O S
H S H O E F I S A S C L R X

or, on graph paper:

| | T | | E | | C | | O | | N | | R | | L | | E | | F | | L | | E | | O | | O | | S | |
| | | H | | S | | H | | O | | E | | F | | I | | S | | A | | S | | C | | L | | R | | X |

Notice how easy it is to stagger the rows evenly if you use graph paper.

Don't worry about keeping spaces between words when you write the message in rows. You'll be dividing the enciphered message into fake words anyway.

4. Now copy down the top row of letters:

TECONRLEFLEOOS

5. And, right next to it, add the bottom row:

TECONRLEFLEOOSHSHOEFISASCLRX

6. Now divide what you have into fake word groups. It is *very* important for deciphering this cipher not to add any more nulls—so you may have to have word groups of different lengths:

TECON|RLEFL|EOOSH|SHOEF|ISASC|LRX
TECON RLEFL EOOSH SHOEF ISASC LRX

And that's all there is to putting a message into Rail Fence Cipher.

To decipher a Rail Fence message, all you have to do, basically, is repeat the enciphering steps backwards.

Here's one to try to decipher:

SESP RTSH OEHI AIAE CONR

(Notice that this one's in four-letter groups for a change!)

1. Divide the message in half so you can set it up in two staggered rows. There are 20 letters in this message, so you'll have two rows of 10 letters each:

SESP RTSH OE|HI AIAE CONR

2. Now on a piece of lined paper or graph paper write down the first 10 letters, leaving quite a bit of space between them, like this:

S E S P R T S H O E

If you use graph paper, skip a square after each letter:

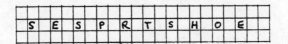

3. Then write the next line underneath, again being sure to stagger it so the first letter of your second line comes *between* the first and second letters of your first line:

S	E	S	P	R	T	S	H	O	E
H	I	A	I	A	E	C	O	N	R

or

	S		E		S		P		R		T		S		H		O		E			
		H		I		A		I		A		E		C		O		N		R		

4. And now copy the message down in a long line, taking one letter from the top row, then one from the bottom, then one from the top, and so on till you're done. (Draw an arrow as you go if it helps.)

S	E	S	P	R	T	S	H	O	E
H	I	A	I	A	E	C	O	N	R

SHEISAPIRATESCHOONER

5. And now go through the message slowly, the way you deciphered Backwards Message Cipher, to pick out the words that make sense. Again, you may have to work at this for a while before you get it right:

SHEISAPIRATESCHOONER

or

SHE IS A PIRATE SCHOONER

After a while, you won't really have to go through all those steps to decipher a simple Rail Fence Cipher. It's a good idea to use them at first, because they'll help you understand how the cipher works. But when you're sure you understand that, you can use this shortcut:

1. Divide the message in half. (You can ignore the spaces between the letters.)

2. Write down the first letter in the first half, followed by the first letter in the second half, followed by the second letter in the first half, followed by the second letter in the second half—and so on, till you have all the letters:

SHEISAPIRATESCHOONER

—and there you have it!

Again, here are a couple for practice:
1. ENcipher:

SHE HIDES HER JOLLY ROGER

2. DEcipher:

SIHAC ONROE ALOSH OECMS

(The answers begin on page 23.)

The other cipher in this chapter—another transposition cipher—is often called Twisted Paths. It's also one of the most fun. Twisted Paths takes a little time to set up, because you have to draw a diagram for it—but most people think it's worth the time.

Here's how Twisted Paths works:

The first thing you do is divide your real message—*before* you encipher it this time—into five-letter groups. If your message is:

UNKNOWN SCHOONER SIGHTED FLYING BRITISH FLAG

it would look like this after being divided:

UNKNO WNSCH OONER SIGHT EDFLY INGBR ITISH FLAGX

(Notice the null added to make the last "word" five letters long.)

You could of course go ahead and just send the message that way, but it probably wouldn't fool anyone for very long.

The next step is to write the five-letter word groups under each other like this:

U N K N O
W N S C H
O O N E R
S I G H T
E D F L Y
I N G B R
I T I S H
F L A G X

Again, graph paper can make this easier. If you're using plain paper, draw lines between the columns and rows of letters, plus a box around the whole diagram. The result should form a checkerboard, like this:

Now comes the fun part. Starting in *any one* of the four corners, draw a line—a "twisted path"—through your checkerboard, hitting each letter *once and once only*. You can make your line go in any direction you want, just so it doesn't hit any letter more than once.

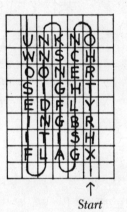

 or

Start

or

Start wherever you like

After you've worked out your path, copy the letters down in the order they appear along your path:

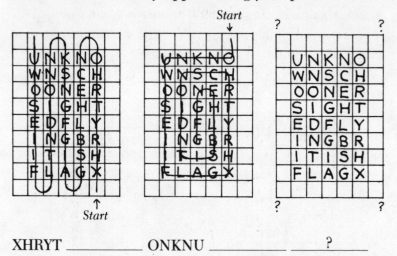

XHRYT _____ ONKNU _____ _____?_____

Make sure to divide your message into five-letter "words" when you've finished enciphering it—or do it as you go along. The enciphered message for the first checkerboard is XHRYT RHONC EHLBS GAIGF GNSKN NOIDN TLFII ESOWU.

For the second, it's ONKNU WOSEI IFLAG XHRYT RHCSN OIDNT ISBLH ENGFG.

And for the third—that's up to you!

Deciphering a Twisted Paths message is almost impossible unless you know the path used for enciphering. So whenever you send a message in Twisted Paths, you must let the receiver of your message know what path you used. If you can be reasonably certain that the message won't be seized by someone who knows the cipher, you could even

draw a little squiggle someplace near the enciphered message to let your friend know the direction of the path:

WHATI PREHS OSITI DNANO THENU
OREBM FHERG TQSNU

To decipher that message according to the path squiggle shown, the first thing to do is count the letters. There
are 40—so what you have to do is make a 40-square checkerboard that measures 5 squares across and enough squares
down to add up to 40 in all:

	1	2	3	4	5	
	6	7	8	9	10	
	11	12	13	14	15	
	16	17	18	19	20	
	21	22	23	24	25	
	26	27	28	29	30	
	31	32	33	34	35	
	36	37	38	39	40	

You know the path goes this way:

So the next step is to draw the path onto your checkerboard:

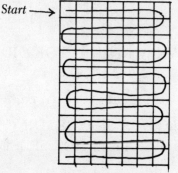

Start ⟶

Now write the enciphered message in the checker-board. Put each letter in its own square in the same order as in the message, but *in the direction of the path:*

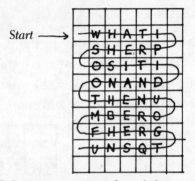

To read the message, read each line in the checkerboard *from left to right* in the ordinary way. If you can't yet make it out, write the letters down in one long line, then divide them up into words that make sense. Here are the first five lines from the checkerboard:

WHATISHERPOSITIONANDTHENU

See if you can write down the rest of the message and then divide it into words. (The completely deciphered message is Number 3 on page 24.)

Here are a couple more Twisted Path ciphers for you to do:

4. DEcipher:

KNOWN NGRWO PFFOR OIUNS
UNOOB TNZOH

5. ENcipher, making up your own path:

WHERE IS SHE HEADING
AND WHAT IS HER SPEED

(The answers are on pages 24 and 25.)

Answers for Chapter Two

1. SEIEH ROLRG RHHDS EJLYO EX

You may have divided the "words" differently. That's okay—just make sure you have the above letters in the order they appear here. You may, of course, have a different null.

Here's how to do it:

SHE HIDES HER JOLLY ROGER

Count the number of letters in the message (21). That's not an even number, so add a null to make it 22 letters. Now you can divide the message in half—into two groups of 11 letters each:

SHEHIDESHER|JOLLYROGER<u>X</u>

Write it in two staggered rows:

S E I E H R O L R G
H H D S E J L Y O E <u>X</u>

To encipher the message, write down the letters from the top row in one long line, and next to that write down the letters from the bottom row. Then divide it into fake "word" groups:

SEIEH|ROLRG|RHHDS|EJLYO|E<u>X</u>

That, as you can see, leaves you with a two-letter "word" at the end. Remember that in this cipher you shouldn't add any more nulls—but you can divide the letters you have into fake "words" of any length you want:

SEIEH ROLRG RHHDS EJLYO E<u>X</u>

or

SE IEH ROLRG RHH DSE JLYOE<u>X</u>

or whatever arrangement you like.

2. The answer is:

SAIL HO A SCHOONER COMES

Here's how it was deciphered:

1. SIHAC ONROE ALOSH OECMS

    20 letters—divides in half after 10 letters:

    SIHACONROE|ALOSHOECMS

2. Write in staggered rows:

    S I H A C O N R O E

     A L O S H O E C M S

3. Read by taking one letter from top, one from bottom, one from top, etc.

3. WHAT IS HER POSITION AND THE NUMBER OF HER GUNS

The letters Q and T are nulls in the cipher.

4. OFF PORT BOW ON HORIZON GUNS UNKNOWN

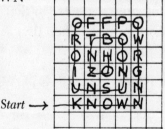

Start →

5. The answer to this one of course depends on the path you used. Here are a couple of possibilities, but you may have another! And you may have used a different null.

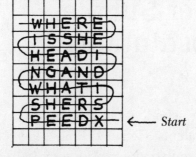

← Start

XDEEP SHERS ITAHW NGAND IDAEH ISSHE EREHW

Start
↓

WIHNW SPEHH GESHE SAAAE EDXSI DIEER HDNTR

3 | Caesar's Ciphers and Other Simple Substitutions

Julius Caesar, who lived in the first century B.C., was a man of many talents. He ruled Rome, led conquering armies, wrote detailed descriptions of battles—and used some very simple but also very clever *substitution ciphers.*

In substitution ciphers you do not scramble letters as you do in transposition ciphers. You keep everything in the original order, but you *replace* each letter of the *alphabet* with another letter, a number, or some kind of drawing. Think of a *substitute* teacher who *replaces* your regular teacher when your regular teacher is sick. In substitution cipher, the real alphabet is like the regular teacher, and the cipher alphabet is like the substitute.

Morse code is a good example of a substitution cipher because in it each letter of the alphabet is replaced by dots, dashes, or both. (Despite its name, Morse is more of a cipher than a code. A few of the dot-dash combinations stand for words, but most people use Morse for enciphering single letters.)

Here is the international Morse alphabet used by ships, with the dots and/or dashes next to the letters they stand for:

A	• −	J	• − − −	S	• • •
B	− • • •	K	− • −	T	−
C	− • − •	L	• − • •	U	• • −
D	− • •	M	− −	V	• • • −
E	•	N	− •	W	• − −
F	• • − •	O	− − −	X	− • • −
G	− − •	P	• − − •	Y	− • − −
H	• • • •	Q	− − • −	Z	− − • •
I	• •	R	• − •		

Samuel Morse invented his "code" nearly 150 years ago for tapping out telegraph messages. But you and a friend can easily exchange Morse messages by flashlight. Use a short flash for a dot, and a longer flash for a dash. Pause a short time between letters and a longer time between words.

You can also write messages in Morse. Just substitute the right group of dots and dashes for the real alphabet letters you need. The word ALPHABET, for example, would be:

A • −
L • − • •
P • − − •
H • • • •
A • −
B ?
E ?
T ?

(Enciphering completed in Number 1 on page 37.)

What would DANGER COMING be in Morse? (The answer is Number 2 on page 38.)

How about:

3. DEcipher

· · ·	· − −	− − −
− · − ·	· ·	· · −
· · · ·	· − · ·	· − ·
− − −	· − · ·	
− − −		− · − ·
− ·	− · − ·	− − −
·	· − ·	· · −
· − ·	− − −	· − ·
	· · ·	· · ·
	·	

4. ENcipher:

BEARING DOWN FAST

(The answers are on page 38.)

Even though Morse is nearly 150 years old, it's fairly modern as ciphers go. Let's move further back in time now and return to Caesar.

Caesar sent his messages in Latin but the ciphers that bear his name can be used in almost any written language. In English, there are twenty-five Caesar ciphers—or Caesar "alphabets," as they are often called.

Here's the first one:

real alphabet⎫ A B C D E F G H I J K L M N O P Q R S T U V W X Y Z

cipher alphabet⎫ B C D E F G H I J K L M N O P Q R S T U V W X Y Z A

To decipher the message:

TDIPP OFSMB VODIJ OHTNB MMCPB UYYZA

all you have to do is:

1. Look in the cipher alphabet for the first letter of the cipher message—T. Put your pencil on that T.

2. Move your pencil point straight up to find what letter that T in the cipher alphabet stands for in the real alphabet. (S, right?) So write S above the first T in the message.

3. Do the same for the other letters in the message. (Don't worry about the spacing yet. As usual, the message has been divided into fake "words.")

4. When you've deciphered all the letters, pick out the real words by reading along the deciphered message till you find words that make sense. Watch out for nulls at the end!

Here's part of the message deciphered, with the first word of the real message picked out for you:

message ⎤
in real ⎬
alphabet ⎦ SCHOO NERLA U
_____
message ⎤ TDIPP OFSMB VODIJ OHTNB MMCPB UYYZA
in cipher ⎬
alphabet ⎦

Can you finish it? (It's deciphered in Number 5 on page 38.)

Notice the nulls in Number 5 when you look up the answer. You'll remember from transposition ciphers that there are things to watch out for when using nulls. In this cipher, what you have to watch out for is that the nulls don't spell anything in the *real* alphabet when those letters have been substituted for the cipher letters. In this cipher, for example, the nulls TUXP would completely change the meaning of the message. Try them as nulls and see! (You can check your answer with Number 6 on page 38.)

To ENcipher a message, you do just the opposite of what you did to DEcipher. Try the word ENCIPHER:

1. Find the first letter of the real message—E—in the real alphabet.

2. Slide your pencil *down* to find out what stands for E in the cipher alphabet. F, right? So write F under the E of your real message.

3. Go on till you have all the letters, and then divide your message into five-letter "words," adding nulls if you need them.

    E N C I P H E R
    F O D J Q I F S

               FODJQ IFS<u>UR</u>

What are the nulls, deciphered? Are they good ones? (The answer is Number 7 on page 38.)

Here are a couple of practice messages in the same Caesar alphabet:

8. ENcipher:

    BOAT HEADING FOR MARY ANN

9. DEcipher:

    MPTUT JHIUP GCPBU JOEBS LRFCU

(The answers are on page 39.)

All 25 Caesar alphabets follow the same pattern. To write one, first write down the real alphabet (graph paper, as always, can be a help):

real alphabet

Then underneath it write the real alphabet again (write it in a different color if you want), only this time start it with any letter *except* A. Write down the letters in order till you get to Z. Then after Z, write A, and go on again in order till you've used all 26 letters.

Here's a Caesar alphabet starting with D. It's the one Caesar himself is said to have used most often:

real alphabet

A	B	C	D	E	F	G	H	I	J	K	L	M	N	O	P	Q	R	S	T	U	V	W	X	Y	Z
D	E	F	G	H	I	J	K	L	M	N	O	P	Q	R	S	T	U	V	W	X	Y	Z	A	B	C

cipher alphabet

Suppose you wanted to send the following message, using the Caesar alphabet cipher that starts with D:

SCHOONER STILL IN SIGHT

Find the first letter in the real message—S—in the real alphabet. Then look down to see what letter it is in the cipher alphabet—V, right? Write that under the S of the real message—on graph paper if you can:

real message: S C H O O N E R   S T I L L   I N   S I G H T
cipher message: V

Then find what the second letter of the real message—
C—is in the cipher alphabet: F.

real message: S C H O O N E R   S T I L L   I N   S I G H T
cipher message: V F

You should be able to finish enciphering the message
now. Remember to divide it into five-letter words and to
add nulls if you need them! (Check your answer with
Number 10 on page 39.)

Remember that you can start a Caesar alphabet with
any letter you want *except* A. Always put A after Z in your
cipher alphabet and go on from there again in order till
you've used all 26 letters.

You and a friend could use a different Caesar alphabet
each day for almost a month. Start your cipher alphabet
with B on the first day, C on the second, and so on. That
way if an unwelcome acquaintance catches on to your
method he or she will still go a little crazy trying to figure
out which alphabet you're using!

Log entry by Captain Joshua Snow
for the coastal trader Mary Ann

September 7. 32°35′N, 80°5′W
Running before a fair easterly wind, but in growing fog,
so we proceed cautiously. We are on course and on time,
despite yesterday's calm and despite stops at several ports.

My crew is restless about the unknown British schooner we have sighted, as indeed am I. She dogs us night and day but keeps to our speed and never comes close enough to hail, although at nightfall yesterday her crew launched a boat. However, we soon lost sight of both ship and boat in the dark. I am in mind uncomfortably of the cipher messages handed me and my mate when we left Charleston— for pirates, I know, often shadow a vessel before boarding, to ensure she is a worthy prize. I have given orders to make all look slovenly aboard should she approach. Though so far the cargo we have taken on is worth little, I know not the contents of those chests which William Pace seemed to value so highly when he put them on board— and the *Mary Ann* herself is a sprightly ship that a pirate might well think a worthy prize.

I think often of my son, who would have shipped with me this voyage, had the fates spared him to me. Alas, I fear his ship *The Pride of Charleston* is lost, for I hear no news in any port of her.

I keep this for last, for it troubles me sore and I know not if it be linked to the schooner that haunts us like a ghost ship. I do not see how it can be, yet I do not see how it can be otherwise explained. Today, when hauling in the lead from taking soundings in dense fog, a man of the starboard watch reported what he termed "queer writings" on our bow. Mister Forther, my first mate, sent a man out on the bowsprit and down a line, and he reported seeing carved shallowly these letters, which I have determined are in simple Backwards Alphabet Cipher, with the words all remaining their true lengths:

HSRK GSLF ZIG WLLNVW

I shudder—yet it is no doubt only foolishness and no connection with the strange schooner—perhaps a prank of some discontented young seaman, or the boy.

Backwards Alphabet Cipher is another easy substitution cipher, similar to the Caesar alphabets. The cipher alphabet is simply the real alphabet backwards:

real
alphabet⌋ A B C D E F G H I J K L M N O P Q R S T U V W X Y Z

cipher
alphabet⌋ Z Y X W V U T S R Q P O N M L K J I H G F E D C B A

Can you figure out why Captain Snow shuddered? (The answer is Number 11 on page 39.)

A somewhat different kind of substitution alphabet is *Half-and-Half Alphabet*. Each half of the real alphabet is the cipher for the other half:

A B C D E F G H I J K L M
N O P Q R S T U V W X Y Z

This cipher is often called Porta's Simple, because it is based on one invented by a sixteenth-century Italian scientist and cipher expert named Giovanni Porta. In it there is a double substitution: A stands for N and N stands for A; B and O stand for each other; C and P stand for each other—and so on:

A B C D E F G H I J K L M
↕ ↕ ↕ ↕ ↕ ↕ ↕ ↕ ↕ ↕ ↕ ↕ ↕
N O P Q R S T U V W X Y Z

SAIL HO would be enciphered:

S A I L   H O

F N V Y   ? ?

(See Number 12 on page 39 for the rest.)

Again, messages in this cipher (and also in Backwards Alphabet Cipher) are usually divided into fake "words," with nulls if needed.

Using Half-and-Half Alphabet:

13. ENcipher:

SHE IS THE SAME SCHOONER

14. DEcipher:

UREOE VGVFU SYNTV FTBAR

(The answers are on pages 39 and 40.)

From the secret diary of Samuel Snow

Sept. 9

We are bearing down fast on a small coastal ship—alas, I fear she is the *Mary Ann*! I wish it meant that rescue were at hand, but I am sure instead it means a greater doom to sadden my poor mother's heart. I have heard the halyards creak above my head and am sure the pirate crew has struck the false British colors that deceived my own captain and led to our capture.— Yes, those telltale lines creak again even as I write, and the Jolly Roger, which to me is not a jolly flag at all but as grim as the skull and bones it darkly shows, is now, I am sure, being run up to the masthead. Woe to the poor small ship and her captain, whoever they may be! Were it only night and had I only a light, I could perhaps signal—were the stranger truly the *Mary Ann* I would signal urgently with the flashes my

father and I made up for the Aabab Cipher, using one flash
for A and two quick ones for B. Could I be sure it was my
father's ship, I would wish to signal thus—for though the
act, if carried out, would endanger me, it might save the
Mary Ann, whose stout crew is equal to battle if unsur-
prised:

aaaaa/baaba/baaba/aaaaa/aaaba/abaab

What Sam Snow called the "Aabab Cipher" is based on
a cipher invented in the sixteenth century by the English
statesman and author Sir Francis Bacon. Bacon's cipher
was quite complicated, but the first of its several steps can
be used by itself as a simple substitution cipher. As you can
see, though, it's too long for all but the shortest messages—
or the most patient of senders and receivers!

Real Alphabet	Cipher Alphabet	Real Alphabet	Cipher Alphabet
A	aaaaa	N	abbaa
B	aaaab	O	abbab
C	aaaba	P	abbba
D	aaabb	Q	abbbb
E	aabaa	R	baaaa
F	aabab	S	baaab
G	aabba	T	baaba
H	aabbb	U, V	baabb
I, J	abaaa	W	babaa
K	abaab	X	babab
L	ababa	Y	babba
M	ababb	Z	babbb

Can you decipher the message Sam wants to send his father? (The answer is Number 15 on page 40.)

You could make up a cipher like this one by using different letters—Loolo Cipher, maybe, or Eezee. Notice that in Bacon's version the same cipher letters stand for I and J, and for U and V. This is true of the updated versions of a number of old ciphers that were originally in Latin. In the Latin (or Roman) alphabet, I and J started out as one letter, and so did U and V.

Here are some messages for practice in Bacon's Aabab Cipher:

16. ENcipher:

BEWARE

17. DEcipher:

aaabb/aaaaa/abbaa/aabba/aabaa/baaaa

(**18.** The answers are abbab/abbaa abbba/aaaaa/ aabba/aabaa 40.)

Answers for Chapter Three

1. A • –
   L • – • •
   P • – – •
   H • • • •
   A • –
   B – • • •
   E •
   T –

2.
D – · ·	C – · – ·
A · –	O – – –
N – ·	M – –
G – – ·	I · ·
E ·	N – ·
R · – ·	G – – ·

3. SCHOONER WILL CROSS OUR COURSE

4.
B – · · ·	D – · ·
E ·	O – – –
A · –	W · – –
R · – ·	N – ·
I · ·	
N – ·	F · · · – ·
G – – ·	A · –
	S · · ·
	T –

5. SCHOONER LAUNCHING SMALL BOAT

SCHOO NERLA UNCHI NGSMA LLBOA TXXYZ
TDIPP OFSMB VODIJ OHTNB MMCPB UYYZA

6. SCHOONER LAUNCHING SMALL BOATS TWO

SCHOO NERLA UNCHI NGSMA LLBOA TSTWO
TDIPP OFSMB VODIJ OHTNB MMCPB UTUXP

7. Yes. The nulls, deciphered, are TQ; they don't spell anything in the real alphabet, so they are all right to use.

8. B O A T   H E A D I N G   F O R   M A R Y   A N N
    C P B U   I|F B E J O|H   G P S   N|B S Z   B O|O

CPBUI FBEJO HGPSN BSZBO O<u>SUAZ</u>

                    (RTZY
                    in the
                    real
                    alphabet)

You, of course, probably have different nulls.

9. LOST SIGHT OF BOAT IN DARK <u>QEBT</u>

    LOSTS   IGHTO F   BOAT   INDAR   KQEBT
    M P T U T   J H I U P   G C P B U   J O E B S   L R F C U

10. VFKRR QHUVW LOOLQ VLJKW

    S C H O O N E R   S T I L L   I N   S I G H T
    V F K R R|Q H U   V W|L O O   L Q| V L J K W
                        (no nulls needed)

11. S H I P   T H O U   A R T   D O O M E D
     H S R K   G S L F   Z I G   W L L N V W

12. S A I L   H O
     F N V Y   U B

13. FURVF GURFN ZRFPU BBARE

    S H E   I S   T H E   S A M E   S C H O O N E R
    F U R   V F   G U R   F N Z R   F P U B B A R E

14. HER BRITISH FLAG IS GONE

HER BR   I T I S H   FLAG I   S GONE
U R E O E   V G V F U   S Y N T V   F T B A R

15. ATTACK

16. aaaab/aabaa/babaa/aaaaa/baaaa/aabaa

   B   E   W   A   R   E
aaaab   aabaa   babaa   aaaaa   baaaa   aabaa

17. DANGER

   D   A   N   G   E   R
aaabb   aaaaa   abbaa   aabba   aabaa   baaaa

18. . . . ON PAGE . . .

4 | When A Is 2— —or 4— —or More!

Log entry by Captain Joshua Snow
for the coastal trader Mary Ann

September 10. Standing off Fripps Island
On the cry of "Sail ho!" simultaneous with the striking of eight bells, I went on deck and beheld the entire watch clustered at the port rail. No wonder, for the schooner that has been dogging us despite our frequent calls in port for trade was now running straight at us before a strong and lively breeze!

I ordered sail piled on to help us flee, but though the sun sparkles merrily on the sea this day, I fear all is not well. Even as I write this I hear cries from above: "She gains— she gains on us!" "She strikes her colors!" and dread fills me so full I almost do not wish to leave my cabin. But this is fainthearted and unfitting—and so I go above.

(Later this same day.)
Going above, I arrive just in time to see the schooner still gaining on us, flying—as I feared—no longer the British flag but the dread Jolly Roger, a white skull and bones on a black field. I bethought me of my cargo and examined it. I set this down here for the owner, Mr. William Pace, to

see my reasons for opening the secret chests: I think that since the cargo now seems under threat of piracy I should know whatof it is that I may the better protect it—or recover it, should it be stolen. And what I have seen increases my fear for its safety, and my ship's safety and that of my crew—for one chest is full of the costliest of jewels, and the other of gold.

I end this now in haste, for I must have my mate Mister Forther prepare all hands for battle.— But even as I wrote the above came Mister Forther in to me, and my heart beats fast with his tidings, for he handed me a paper with numbers written thereon, saying that he has seen a light flashing from the hold of the schooner, as if deflected from a piece of shiny metal. The light flashed, he said, these times in this order: 6 · 1 · 20 · 8 · 5 · 18 · 9 · 1 · 13 · 3 · 1 · 16 · 20 · 9 · 22 · 5 · 8 · 5 · 18 · 5 · 2 · 5 · 23 · 1 · 18 · 5 · 16 · 9 · 18 · 1 · 20 · 5 · 19—which I recognize as perhaps being some message in Forwards Number Cipher, well known both to me and—oh, dare I hope it—my beloved son Samuel!

The pirate ship, gaining though she was, must have been moving fairly slowly to give Samuel time to flash that rather long message to his father: He had to flash his piece of metal 335 times in all!

Forwards Number Cipher is a substitution cipher very much like the Caesar alphabets. The main difference is that numbers are used in the cipher alphabet instead of letters:

real alphabet: A B C D E F G H I J K L M
cipher alphabet: 1 2 3 4 5 6 7 8 9 10 11 12 13

real alphabet: N O P Q R S T U V W X Y Z
cipher alphabet: 14 15 16 17 18 19 20 21 22 23 24 25 26

The important thing to remember if you flash a message in Forwards Number Cipher is to pause a short time between letters and a longer time between words. If you don't, your receiver won't be able to "read" your message at all!

As long as you remember to put dots between the numbers, you can probably write this cipher more easily than you can flash it. You can either write it in one long line, as the mate did, or you can divide it into "words":

6 • 1 • 20 • 8 • 5   18 • 9 • 1 • 13 • 3   1 • 16 • 20 • 9 • 22
5 • 8 • 5 • 18 • 5   2 • 5 • 23 • 1 • 18   5 • 16 • 9 • 18 • 1
20 • 5 • 19 • ____ • ____

Divided into "words," as you can see, it needs two nulls. What would be good ones?

Can you decipher Sam's message? (The answer is Number 1 on page 52.)

Here's another message in a number cipher—one called *Backwards* Number Cipher. A is 26, B is 25, C is 24, and so on. Write down the real alphabet with the cipher alphabet beneath it. (Graph paper, as always, is a help in lining up the letters and numbers.) Then see if you can decipher the message. If you *don't* use graph paper, be sure to leave enough space between the letters so you'll have room to write the numbers under them without squeezing!

4 · 22 · 4 · 18 · 15 · 15 · 21 · 18 · 20 · 19 · 7 · 7 · 18 · 15 · 15 · 7 · 26 · 16 · 22 · 13

(The answer is Number 2 on page 52.)

Here are a couple more. Be careful to notice which cipher to use for each one!

3. ENcipher, in Backwards Number Cipher:

THE PIRATES HAVE MORE GUNS

4. DEcipher (the message is in Forwards Number Cipher):

20 · 15 · 20 · 8 · 5   18 · 1 · 9 · 12 · 16   9 · 18 · 1 · 20 · 5
19 · 2 · 15 · 1 · 18   4 · 9 · 14 · 7 · 23

(Answers are on pages 52 and 53.)

Working with the next cipher—Checkerboard Number cipher—is a little like looking up the name of a city in a map index. Say you wanted to find the city of Omaha on a map. In the index, you might find something like "Omaha —27 D 3." To find where Omaha is, you turn to the map on page 27, find the letter D at the top of the page and the number 3 on the side. You run one finger in a straight line down from D and another finger in a straight line over from 3 and where your fingers meet, you should find the city of Omaha.

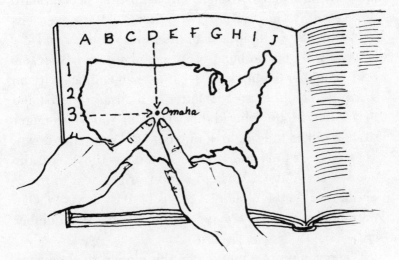

That same principle is used in Checkerboard Number Cipher. In that cipher, each letter of the real alphabet is replaced by a two-digit number, like 13, 25, or 42.

To use Checkerboard Number Cipher, first draw a checkerboard that looks like this (use graph paper if you want):

	1	2	3	4	5
1	A	B	C	D	E
2	F	G	H	I	J
3	K	L	M	N	O
4	P	Q	R	S	T
5	U	V	W	xz	Y

Since there are only 25 squares, you have to double up on one pair of letters. You could choose I and J, or U and V, as in Bacon's Aabab Cipher. Or, as in the checkerboard above, you could combine two letters that are even less likely than those to appear in the same word—X and Z.

Once you get the hang of it, enciphering in Checkerboard Number Cipher is even easier than finding a city on a map. To encipher the real letter H, for example, first find that letter in the checkerboard. Then run your finger straight out to the side to a number—2. Write that down. Then go back to H and straight up from it till you hit the number above it—3. Write that down right next to the 2. The letter H in this cipher is 23. A is 11, B is 12; S is 44. One warning: be sure you *always* write down the *side* number first.

When you write a message in this cipher, remember to put dots between the numbers to keep them separate.

5. DEcipher (X and Z are together in one square):

44 · 45 · 11 · 34 · 14   14 · 35 · 22 · 44 · 11
34 · 14 · 21 · 24 · 22   23 · 45 · 42 · 43 · 21

6. ENcipher, but this time put I and J in the same square:

PRISON OR THE PLANK

(Answers are on pages 53 and 54.)

Here's another to try. If it doesn't seem right, maybe you've doubled up on the wrong letters. (Either X and Z, I and J, or U and V are in the same square.)

```
24  43 • 11 • 32 • 45 • 15 • 31   52 • 42 • 24 • 44 • 15
44 • 23 • 24 • 43   24 • 33   13 • 24 • 35 • 23 • 15 • 42
31 • 15 • 43 • 44   24 • 44   12 • 15
14 • 24 • 43 • 13 • 34 • 51 • 15 • 42 • 15 • 14   44 • 23 • 15
32 • 11 • 42 • 54   11 • 33 • 33   24 • 43
13 • 11 • 35 • 44 • 45 • 42 • 15 • 14   11 • 33 • 14   32 • 54
21 • 11 • 44 • 23 • 15 • 42   52 • 24 • 44 • 23   23 • 15 • 42
11 • 33 • 14   44 • 23 • 15   35 • 24 • 42 • 11 • 44 • 15
43 • 13 • 23 • 34 • 34 • 33 • 15 • 42   33 • 34 • 52
43 • 11 • 24 • 31 • 43   21 • 34 • 42   52 • 15   25 • 33 • 34 • 52
33 • 34 • 44   52 • 23 • 11 • 44   35 • 34 • 42 • 44   24
23 • 15 • 11 • 42   44 • 11 • 31 • 25   34 • 21   11 • 33
24 • 43 • 31 • 11 • 33 • 14   14 • 45 • 33 • 22 • 15 • 34 • 33
11 • 31 • 11 • 43
```

(See number 7 on page 54 for this message.)

Log entry by Captain Joshua Snow
for the coastal trader Mary Ann
September 16 (?). Position unknown

What stronghold we are in I know not, but this I know (for I loosened my blindfold enough to see): The pirates have taken us to an island and thrown us into a dungeon in which are many cells already occupied by other prisoners. By *us* I mean my officers and crew as well as myself, plus the prisoners they had on board the schooner—my beloved son among them, whom I am greatly glad to see alive—but we had time for only the briefest of embraces before, alas, again they separated us. The pirates have taken the tobacco in my hold for their own pleasure; the ribbons they have used to decorate their already outlandish garb; my ship's food they will doubtless consume—and they have taken the two chests deep into the jungle on this island, where I suppose they will bury them. I write this "log" on paper hastily torn from my old log as it was wrenched from me by the pirate captain—how I regret I did not keep the whole of it in cipher, for he will know the contents of those two chests! I must therefore keep this account short, for I have little paper, and know not how long it will be ere I can escape—for escape I must, to free my son, my crew, and the other wretched prisoners, and to recover the cargo. I will send a message in Russian Tap Cipher to the next cell tonight and see if I may learn where Sam is prisoner. We must turn our minds to escape, Sam and I, and to freeing the others, and to the recovery of the chests William Pace entrusted to my care.

And now I shall fold this paper—I have written so small I have used only part of a single sheet—and slide it into my boot's secret heel compartment for safekeeping.

Tap ciphers, like the one Captain Snow says he is planning to use, have long been a favorite means of communication among prisoners, who don't usually have pen or paper, or lights to flash, but who do often have a hard object—a stone, a spoon—to tap with and a surface shared with someone else—a cell wall—to tap on. Many ciphers can be tapped. Morse is one, as you know, and Bacon's Aabab Cipher is another (use one tap for a and two for b). Any time you use a tap cipher, no matter which one it is, remember to pause briefly between letters in order to keep them separate, and to pause a little longer between words.

Like Morse, the cipher that Captain Snow called "Russian Tap Cipher" was designed for tapping. Some experts say it was used in Russia in the late 1800s by people who were put in jail for being against the czar (emperor) and his government.

To send a message in this cipher, first write down the checkerboard you used for Checkerboard Number Cipher (if you're in a dungeon, you can draw it on the dirt floor, or scratch it onto stone with another stone or a spoon—or even just "write" it in your mind):

	1	2	3	4	5	
1	A	B	C	D	E	
2	F	G	H	I	J	
3	K	L	M	N	O	
4	P	Q	R	S	T	
5	U	V	W	xz	Y	

When you send a message, you tap the two numbers for each letter instead of writing them down. The number for A—11—is tapped out with one tap followed by another tap—1-1, rather than 11. The number for B is one tap followed by two taps —1-2 . The tricky part, of course, is the pauses. You have to have a short pause between the first and second number for each letter. You also have to pause—a little longer—after each letter, and longer still after each word.

The first word of the message WHERE IS SAM SNOW is tapped out this way:

tap-tap-tap-tap-tap	—pause— LONGER PAUSE	tap-tap-tap	W (5-3)
tap-tap	—pause— LONGER PAUSE	tap-tap-tap	H (2-3)
tap	—pause— LONGER PAUSE	tap-tap-tap-tap-tap	E (1-5)
tap-tap-tap-tap	—pause— LONGER PAUSE	tap-tap-tap	R (4-3)
tap	—pause— VERY LONG PAUSE (to show end of word)	tap-tap-tap-tap-tap	E (1-5)

Can you finish tapping the message? (The answer is Number 8 on page 54.)

To practice Tap Cipher:

9. ENcipher:

I AM HERE

10. DEcipher:

tap	—pause— LONGER PAUSE	tap-tap-tap-tap
tap-tap	—pause— LONGER PAUSE	tap-tap-tap-tap
tap-tap	—pause— VERY LONG PAUSE	tap-tap
tap-tap-tap	—pause— LONGER PAUSE	tap-tap-tap-tap-tap
tap-tap-tap-tap-tap	—pause— LONGER PAUSE	tap

tap-tap-tap-tap	—pause—	tap-tap-tap-tap-tap
	VERY LONG PAUSE	
tap-tap-tap-tap	—pause—	tap-tap-tap-tap-tap
	LONGER PAUSE	
tap-tap-tap	—pause—	tap-tap-tap-tap-tap
	LONGER PAUSE	
tap-tap-tap	—pause—	tap-tap-tap
	LONGER PAUSE	
tap-tap-tap	—pause—	tap-tap-tap-tap-tap
	LONGER PAUSE	
tap-tap-tap-tap	—pause—	tap-tap-tap
	LONGER PAUSE	
tap-tap-tap-tap	—pause—	tap-tap-tap
	LONGER PAUSE	
tap-tap-tap	—pause—	tap-tap-tap-tap-tap
	LONGER PAUSE	
tap-tap-tap-tap-tap	—pause—	tap-tap-tap
	VERY LONG PAUSE	
tap-tap-tap	—pause—	tap-tap-tap-tap
	LONGER PAUSE	
tap-tap	—pause—	tap-tap-tap-tap
	LONGER PAUSE	
tap-tap	—pause—	tap-tap
	LONGER PAUSE	
tap-tap	—pause—	tap-tap-tap
	LONGER PAUSE	
tap-tap-tap-tap	—pause—	tap-tap-tap-tap-tap
	(End of Message)	

(Answers are on pages 55 and 56.)

Answers for Chapter Four

1. FATHER I AM CAPTIVE HERE BEWARE PI-RATES
Good nulls would be any two numbers that don't spell a word.

2. WE WILL FIGHT TILL TAKEN
Backwards Number Cipher:

real alphabet: A B C D E F G H I J K L M
cipher alphabet: 26 25 24 23 22 21 20 19 18 17 16 15 14

real alphabet: N O P Q R S T U V W X Y Z
cipher alphabet: 13 12 11 10 9 8 7 6 5 4 3 2 1

W E W I L L F I G H T
4 · 22 · 4 · 18 · 15 · 15 · 21 · 18 · 20 · 19 · 7 ·

T I L L T A K E N
7 · 18 · 15 · 15 · 7 · 26 · 16 · 22 · 13

3. 7·19·22·11·18 9·26·7·22·8
19·26·5·22·14 12·9·22·20·6
13·8·14·13·25
Remember—this one was *Backwards* Number Cipher:

T H E P I R A T E S H A
7 · 19 · 22 · 11 · 18 · 9 · 26 · 7 · 22 · 8 · 19 · 26 ·

V E M O R E G U N S M N B
5 · 22 · 14 · 12 · 9 · 22 · 20 · 6 · 13 · 8 · 14 · 13 · 25

You probably have other nulls. It's also okay if you didn't divide the message into five-letter "words." That's really up to you, now that you know what you're doing. You might like four-letter "words" better, or three, or some other number that will disguise the real lengths of the words in your message. You might even want to experiment with a mixture—for example, four-letter "words" alternating with three-letter "words," or even "words" of random lengths. Experiment all you like! Just remember to let your partner know what you're doing.

4. TO THE RAIL PIRATES BOARDING
   This one is in *Forwards* Number Cipher:

T O T H E R A I L P I R A
20 · 15 · 20 · 8 · 5 · 18 · 1 · 9 · 12 · 16 · 9 · 18 · 1 ·

T E S B O A R D I N G W
20 · 5 · 19 · 2 · 15 · 1 · 18 · 4 · 9 · 14 · 7 · 23

5. STAND DOGS AND FIGHT

	1	2	3	4	5
1	A	B	C	D	E
2	F	G	H	I	J
3	K	L	M	N	O
4	P	Q	R	S	T
5	U	V	W	xz	Y

S	T	A	N	D	D	O	G	S	A
44 ·	45 ·	11 ·	34 ·	14	14 ·	35 ·	22 ·	44 ·	11

N	D	F	I	G	H	T	Q	R	F
34 ·	14 ·	21 ·	24 ·	22	23 ·	45 ·	42 ·	43 ·	21

6. Remember that the checkerboard has I and J in the same square!

   35 · 42 · 24 · 43 · 34 33 · 34 · 42 · 44 · 23
   15 · 35 · 31 · 11 · 33 25 · 11 · 21 · 22 · 23

   Again, your nulls will probably be different.

7. I and J are in the same square.

   I Samuel write this in cipher lest it be discovered. The Mary Ann is captured and my father with her, and the pirate schooner now sails for we know not what port. I hear talk of an island dungeon. Alas.

   (Sam didn't show the punctuation. That's usually very hard—often impossible—to do in cipher. It's also often dangerous, because it can help an enemy to decipher.)

8.

tap-tap-tap-tap-tap	—pause—	tap-tap-tap	W (5–3)
	LONGER PAUSE		
tap-tap	—pause—	tap-tap-tap	H (2–3)
	LONGER PAUSE		
tap	—pause—	tap-tap-tap-tap-tap	E (1–5)
	LONGER PAUSE		
tap-tap-tap-tap	—pause—	tap-tap-tap	R (4–3)
	LONGER PAUSE		

tap	—pause—	tap-tap-tap-tap-tap	E	(1–5)
	VERY LONG PAUSE			
tap-tap	—pause—	tap-tap-tap-tap	I	(2–4)
	LONGER PAUSE			
tap-tap-tap-tap	—pause—	tap-tap-tap-tap	S	(4–4)
	VERY LONG PAUSE			
tap-tap-tap-tap	—pause—	tap-tap-tap-tap	S	(4–4)
	LONGER PAUSE			
tap	—pause—	tap	A	(1–1)
	LONGER PAUSE			
tap-tap-tap	—pause—	tap-tap-tap	M	(3–3)
	VERY LONG PAUSE			
tap-tap-tap-tap	—pause—	tap-tap-tap-tap	S	(4–4)
	LONGER PAUSE			
tap-tap-tap	—pause—	tap-tap-tap-tap	N	(3–4)
	LONGER PAUSE			
tap-tap-tap	—pause—	tap-tap-tap-tap-tap	O	(3–5)
	LONGER PAUSE			
tap-tap-tap-tap-tap	—pause—	tap-tap-tap	W	(5–3)
	(End of Message)			

9.

tap-tap	—pause—	tap-tap-tap-tap	I	(2–4)
	VERY LONG PAUSE			
tap	—pause—	tap	A	(1–1)
	LONGER PAUSE			
tap-tap-tap	—pause—	tap-tap-tap	M	(3–3)
	VERY LONG PAUSE			
tap-tap	—pause—	tap-tap-tap	H	(2–3)
	LONGER PAUSE			
tap	—pause—	tap-tap-tap-tap-tap	E	(1–5)
	LONGER PAUSE			

tap-tap-tap-tap	—pause—	tap-tap-tap	R (4–3)
	LONGER PAUSE		
tap	—pause—	tap-tap-tap-tap-tap	E (1–5)
	(End of Message)		

10.

D I G O U T T O M O
1–4 · 2–4 · 2–2   3–5 · 5–1 · 4–5   4–5 · 3–5 · 3–3 · 3–5 ·

R R O W N I G H T
4–3 · 4–3 · 3–5 · 5–3   3–4 · 2–4 · 2–2 · 2–3 · 4–5

1 tap plus 4 taps—1–4—D
2 taps plus 4 taps—2–4—I
2 taps plus 2 taps—2–2—G

etc.

5 | Pigpen, Ancient Ogham, and Other Secret Alphabets

1   2   3

In a way, all the drawings above are codes, because they all communicate messages without using words. If you wanted to use words instead of pictures to communicate the messages shown on these signs, what words would you use? (The answers are Numbers 1, 2, and 3 on page 69.)

Each picture is a kind of code *symbol* for its message, the way a red flag is a symbol for danger, and a drawing of a fluffy cotton blossom on a map is a symbol for the message "Cotton is grown here." A symbol is something—it can be almost anything—that stands for something else. The letters and numbers of the substitution alphabets you've been reading about are symbols; they stand for the letters of the real alphabet. But usually when people talk about symbols in cipher or code, they mean some kind of drawing that stands for a letter (cipher), or for a word or phrase (code).

The alphabets you'll read about in this chapter are all substitution cipher alphabets, but they all use picture symbols instead of letters or numbers.

Cipher symbols range from the simple dots and dashes of Morse to elaborate drawings. You can easily invent a brand-new cipher alphabet by making up your own symbols. Just write the real alphabet on a clean sheet of paper, and after each letter draw anything you want:

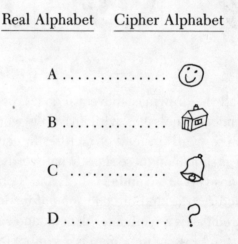

Real Alphabet   Cipher Alphabet

A . . . .

B . . . .

C . . . .

D . . . .

As soon as you have a different drawing for each letter of the alphabet, you have your own personal substitution cipher. You could make up a code in the same way, using symbols to stand for words and phrases you need to use:

Real Word(s)	Code Symbol

I'm late! . . . .

It's my birthday. . . . .

My dog is sick. . . . .

What's the homework? . . . .

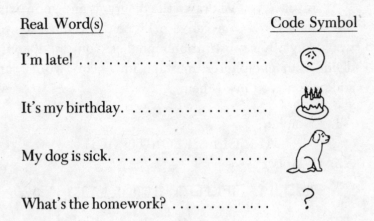

—and so on.

Down through history, people have made up their own cipher alphabets using symbols other than letters or numbers.

Here's an old substitution cipher that looks especially mysterious, even though most people call it by an ordinary-sounding name: Pigpen! To write down the Pigpen alphabet, you first put all the letters in little fence-like diagrams like these:

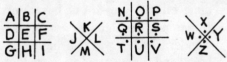

Don't forget the dots in the last two diagrams!

The cipher symbol for each letter is the part of the diagram in which it appears:

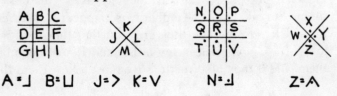

Again, once you've drawn the diagrams and know what the symbols are, you can use Pigpen just the way you would any other substitution alphabet. You can of course divide your enciphered message into fake "words" and add nulls as you need them.

4. ENcipher:
> ALL CLEAR FOR TONIGHT

5. DEcipher:

> ⌐⊔⊐⅃< ⌐⌐⅃⊡⊐ ⊐⊐⊔⅃⅃⊏⊐⅃ ∧⅃⅃

(The answers are on page 69.)

From the secret diary of Samuel Snow

Sept. 17, by my reckoning

Oh, wonder of all wonders that my father shares this dungeon with me—for he has tapped to me his identity in cipher, and his plans for escape as well. And now another wonder: Today while bringing me my meal of moldy bread and stale water, my guard let fall a mysterious map that I suspect may show where the pirates have buried the treasure from my father's ship! The map, which I copy here, contains words in what appears to be my old friend Pigpen Cipher, known also in older days as Freemasons' or simple Box and Dot. The cipher words appear to be directions—I fervently hope they are, and that they lead not into a trap. Nonetheless, my father and I must decipher them, and if they be directions we must follow them this very night, when we will at last dig out of this foul dungeon or—I shudder—die in the attempt, for the pirates, I am sure, will not spare us if they find us out.

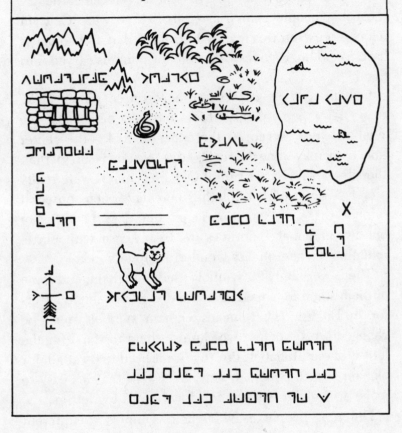

What route will Sam and his father follow if they manage to escape? Decipher the directions on the map yourself—you can check the message in Number 6 on page 70.

The next cipher alphabet in this chapter is called Ogham. The Ogham alphabet we'll use is based on one that was invented in the fourth century or even earlier by the tribal people known as Celts. There were Celts in many places, but it is mainly in Ireland that archeologists have found huge stones with Ogham symbols carved into them.

Ogham symbols are written across a center line, like this: ⵣ . Some people think that may be because the symbols were carved on the edges of rocks—the center line, then, may show the rock's edge. No one is sure of that, though—nor is anyone sure if Ogham symbols were really secret. Many experts think they may have been nonsecret symbols that were sometimes enciphered, as the letters of our own alphabet sometimes are. In any case, with a little updating, Ogham makes wonderful ciphers today.

There were only 20 symbols used in Ogham, and some of them stood for sounds that we don't have single letters for in English. That means Ogham symbols must be changed a little before we can use them to stand for the letters of our alphabet. But that's not hard to do at all, for Ogham is such a logical, sensible system that it's easy to make up Ogham-like symbols for the missing letters.

Different people draw Ogham symbols in different ways. Some people draw them from left to right, like this:

instead of up and down, like this:

Ogham symbols carved in stone.
Photo courtesy of the Irish Tourist Board (Bord Failte photo)

Some people use dots in addition to lines. There's no real right or wrong about it. It's just a matter of interpretation and of different people's ways of bringing Ogham up to date.

Here's an Ogham alphabet that's easy to use for English:

What would the following message be, deciphered?

(The answer is Number 7 on page 70.)

Here are some more:

8. ENcipher:

FIRST WE MUST DIG OUT

(The answer is on page 70.)

9. DEcipher the message at the end of this log entry:

---

*Log entry by Captain Joshua Snow
for the coastal trader* Mary Ann

*September 18 (date estimated but with
agreement among us).*
Position unknown

I write this under a palm tree in the blessed open air, for we have at last dug free! The pirates would surely have

---

noticed had they not been stupefied with sleep from making merry. My son Samuel and I are at last reunited. He looks thin, poor lad, but he is alive and we are together and so I give deep and joyful thanks. We have now freed several of my men and several from Sam's sad ship, and with this band we will seek the chests. If we find them, we will rehide them to keep them from the pirates and then return to the dungeon and free the remaining men. With more men, we hope to overcome the pirates, seize a vessel, and leave this cursed island, taking with us from its new hiding place the rightful property of Mr. William Pace—the chests.

Today at first light we deciphered the Pigpen on the map Sam's guard dropped, and we see from it that the land hereabouts is full of hazards! We have now safely traveled the path shown by the map to the place where the X on most pirate maps would show where treasure is buried. But at the spot marked X, alas, we find only some large monumentlike stones, carved with curious writing. It puts me in mind of an ancient Irish writing of which I have heard. I have only slight memory of how this writing works, but with Samuel's help, I think I can figure it out. It looks like this:

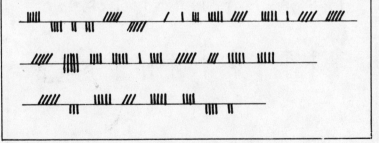

(Message on stone is deciphered in Number 9 on page 71.)

From the secret diary of Samuel Snow

Sept. 18, or thereabouts

I take up this tale where my father left it off, for having at last puzzled out what my father rightly recalled as like the ancient Irish writing called Ogham, we went, as instructed, eighty paces east to the dead tree, where we did indeed dig, but only to find this, which appears to be a practice drawing of pine trees:

—no chests, no treasure.

My father suspects the drawing may be cipher too, or ancient writing, but I fear this may no longer matter, for the pirates now pursue us, and we must flee. Our hope is to elude them this night, and at dawn make our way to the coast and contrive a boat—we will be far from where the ships, our own and theirs, are moored, for we have already been forced to flee far inland. And so on some raft or hand-hewn barge we hope to escape to some friendly vessel and then return, armed and with more men, to take this pirate stronghold.

And now my father calls, excitedly waving the drawing.

Sam's father of course was right about the pine trees. They were symbols from a cipher based on ancient Scandinavian writings called *runes*. Runes were carved onto jewelry and weapons, used for writing religious inscriptions and poetry—they may even have been used in attempts at magic! There are many different runic alphabets and, like Ogham, they were not necessarily secret to begin with. Like Ogham also, runic alphabets make good ciphers today, though they, too, need to be changed a little, since their symbols don't exactly correspond to our letters.

Although there are many different runic alphabets, most of them have two things in common. One is the appearance of the symbols. They can look like this: 𐌀 or this: 𐌗 or even this: ᚱ , but they almost always have straight lines and sharp angles. The other thing many runic alphabets have in common is that each letter of the real alphabet is enciphered according to a *group* number and a number showing the letter's *position* within that group.

The symbol is drawn to show those two numbers in some way.

You can use the Checkerboard Number Cipher checkerboard to give each letter of the real alphabet its group and position number. Group numbers are at the left-hand side of the checkerboard, and position numbers are at the top:

Position Number

Group
Number

	1	2	3	4	5
1	A	B	C	D	E
2	F	G	H	I	J
3	K	L	M	N	O
4	P	Q	R	S	T
5	U	V	W	xz	Y

You know that B in Checkerboard Number Cipher would be 12—and that it would be 1–2 in Tap Cipher. Now think of the first number as the group number and the second as the position number. B is then group 1, position 2. L is group 3, position 2. To draw pine tree runes for those letters, put the branches showing group number on the left, and those showing position number on the right—like this:

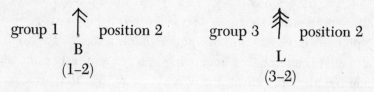

group 1   position 2   group 3   position 2

B   L

(1–2)   (3–2)

and so on.

You should now be able to read the tree drawing, although you might find it easier if you wrote out the whole tree rune alphabet first. (The answer and the alphabet are in Number 10 on page 71.)

Here are a couple more for you to do:

11. DEcipher:

12. ENcipher:

PRESS ON REGARDLESS

(Answers are on pages 72 and 73.)

Answers for Chapter Five

1. STOP
2. NO SMOKING
3. SCHOOL CROSSING

   or

   CHILDREN CROSSING

4. ALL CLEAR FOR TONIGHT

5. TODAY GUARD DROPPED MAP

   TODAY GUARD DROPPED MAP

6.

7. WE WILL FOLLOW THE MAP

8. FIRST WE MUST

DIG OUT

9. EIGHTY PACES EAST TO DEAD TREE THERE DIG

E I G H T Y P A C E S E A S T

T O D E A D T R E E

T H E R E D I G

10. YOU ARE A FOOL WHO FINDS THIS WE DO NOT TELL WHERE TREASURE LIES

Here's the checkerboard again:

Position Number

Group Number

	1	2	3	4	5
1	A	B	C	D	E
2	F	G	H	I	J
3	K	L	M	N	O
4	P	Q	R	S	T
5	U	V	W	XZ	Y

And here's the alphabet:

A	B	C	D	E
Group 1—Position 1	Group 1—Pos. 2	1–3	1–4	1–5

F	G	H	I	J	K	L	M	N	O
2–1	2–2	2–3	2–4	2–5	3–1	3–2	3–3	3–4	3–5

P	Q	R	S	T	U	V	W	XZ	Y
4–1	4–2	4–3	4–4	4–5	5–1	5–2	5–3	5–4	5–5

And the message, deciphered:

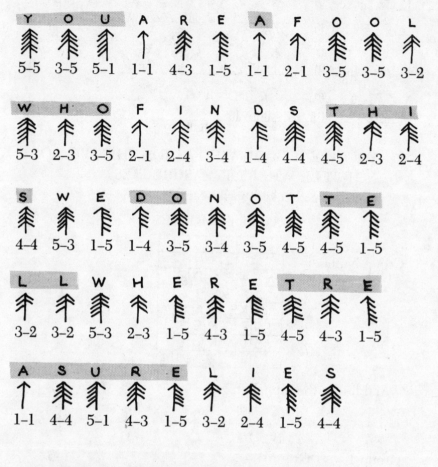

Y	O	U	A	R	E	A	F	O	O	L
5-5	3-5	5-1	1-1	4-3	1-5	1-1	2-1	3-5	3-5	3-2

W	H	O	F	I	N	D	S	T	H	I
5-3	2-3	3-5	2-1	2-4	3-4	1-4	4-4	4-5	2-3	2-4

S	W	E	D	O	N	O	T	T	E
4-4	5-3	1-5	1-4	3-5	3-4	3-5	4-5	4-5	1-5

L	L	W	H	E	R	E	T	R	E
3-2	3-2	5-3	2-3	1-5	4-3	1-5	4-5	4-3	1-5

A	S	U	R	E	L	I	E	S
1-1	4-4	5-1	4-3	1-5	3-2	2-4	1-5	4-4

11. WHAT A DIRTY TRICK

WHAT A DIRTY

TRICK

12.

P R E S S O N R E

4–1 4–3 1–5 4–4 4–4 3–5 3–4 4–3 1–5

G A R D L E S S

2–2 1–1 4–3 1–4 3–2 1–5 4–4 4–4

6 | Mix and Match: Ciphers Plus Codes

By now you're probably pretty clear on the difference between ciphers and codes: In ciphers the symbols stand for single letters. In codes, they stand for entire words or phrases. Codes can sometimes be quicker to use than ciphers. It would be easier, for example, to use one word—TURKEY, say—to stand for the phrase ATTACK AT DAWN than to write the whole message out in cipher. But longer messages can be a problem. To encode, you need an alphabetical list of all the real words and phrases you might want to use in a real message, plus the code words that replace them. And to decode, you need an alphabetical list of code words along with the real words they stand for. A really complete code book for a substitution-type code could end up being larger than a huge unabridged dictionary.

You don't, of course, need a code book for messages in which the real words are rearranged. During the U.S. Civil War, the Union Army used a transposition-type code in which the real words of the message were scrambled into nonsense.

The first step in sending a secret message in Civil War Code is to write out the original message, plus the words

"period" and "question mark" as those marks appear.
(Never mind the other punctuation marks.) Write the message down first in the ordinary way, and then copy it into up-and-down columns, making each column five words long. Add null words to the last column if you need to.

Real Message

To Captain John Steere
Aboard the Flying Fish
Coastal trader Mary Ann missing and believed captured by pirate schooner. Has been glimpsed near Diablo Island with strange crew. Set out at once to rescue and recover valuable cargo.

From William Pace, Owner

(Ships' names, as you may know, are usually printed in italics—*slanted letters*. But that would be a dead giveaway in a code, so they're not in italics here.)

The Message in Columns

To	the	Mary	captured	Has	Island	Set	rescue	period
Captain	Flying	Ann	by	been	with	out	and	From
John	Fish	missing	pirate	glimpsed	strange	at	recover	William
Steere	Coastal	and	schooner	near	crew	once	valuable	Pace
Aboard	trader	believed	period	Diablo	period	to	cargo	owner

Now all you have to do to finish encoding the message is write the words once more, this time as they appear in the columns as you read across from left to right:

The Message Encoded

To the Mary captured Has Island Set rescue period
Captain Flying Ann by been with out and From John
Fish missing pirate glimpsed strange at recover
William Steere Coastal and schooner near crew once
valuable Pace Aboard trader believed period Diablo
period to cargo owner

If you want, you can change some of the capitalizations
to make the encoded message even harder to decode.

To decode a message like this, you have to know the
number of words the sender has put in each column. Many
people use five words to the column. It's okay to use some
other number, but make sure the receiver of your message
knows how many words per column you've used.

To decode:

1. Count the number of words in the message—includ-
ing "period" and "question mark." Then divide by 5 (or
whatever number of words per column you're using). The
answer you get will tell you how many columns to set up.
The message we've been working on has 45 words.

$$\frac{9}{5/45}$$

That means you'll set up 9 columns.

2. Set up the 9 columns by writing the first 9 words
across the top of a clean piece of paper, leaving space
between them, like this:

To   the   Mary   captured Has   Island Set   rescue   period

3. Then write the next 9 words under the first 9, and the
next 9 under them, and so on till you're done:

To	the	Mary	captured	Has	Island	Set	rescue	period
Captain	Flying	Ann	by	been	with	out	and	From
John	Fish	missing	pirate	glimpsed	strange	at	recover	William
Steere	Coastal	and	schooner	near	crew	once	valuable	Pace
Aboard	trader	believed	period	Diablo	period	to	cargo	owner

And there's your message! Just read down the left column, then down the second column, and so on.

Here are a couple more:
1. ENcode:
   To William Pace owner of Mary Ann
   Setting out now for Diablo Island. Please inform
   me as to nature of valuable cargo if possible.
   John Steere, Flying Fish

2. DEcode (5 words per column):
   To Fish jewels period and caution Captain Valuable
   and Also ribbons period John cargo one less period
   Pace Steere one chest important Use dog Flying chest
   gold tobacco great cat

(Answers are on page 83.)

Another way to use this code is to combine it with the system used in Twisted Paths Cipher. To do that, set up your columns as before and then make a "path" through the words, to use as a guide to scrambling. Here's the first message again, set up in columns with a twisted path:

Start

↓

To	the	Mary	captured	Has	Island	Set	rescue	period
Captain	Flying	Ann	by	been	with	out	and	From
John	Fish	missing	pirate	glimpsed	strange	at	recover	William
Steere	Coastal	and	schooner	near	crew	once	valuable	Pace
Abboard	trader	believed	period	Diablo	period	to	cargo	owner

What secret message does that path make? (The answer is Number 3 on page 84.)

The next code, Code Word Substitution, is a more common code—but it's the kind you need a code book for. Instead of scrambling the words of the real message, you replace them with other words, the way you replace letters in substitution ciphers. Usually you only replace the really important words.

For example, this message:

Miss Blue is sailing Thursday from New York.
We would like everyone in the Smith family
who is nearby to meet her at the dock.
Plan for a big party.

takes on a whole new meaning if you know that:

> *Miss Blue* means *the pirate schooner*
> *New York* means *Diablo Island*
> *Smith family* means *navy*
> *the dock* means *Diablo Island Bay*
> *party* means *attack*

What does the message about Miss Blue really mean? (The answer is Number 4 on page 84.)

Try picking out the important words in this message and then substituting other words for them. You can either substitute words that make sense—or completely silly words.

> Only two navy ships are near Diablo Island.
> They will leave immediately to attack the
> pirate stronghold.

(A couple of possible code versions of this message are in Number 5 on page 85.)

Speaking of Diablo Island . . .

---

*Log entry by Captain Joshua Snow
for the coastal trader* Mary Ann

*Estimated date: September 20.
Position: near island coast*

Why I call this poor thing the *Mary Ann*'s log I know not, since my ship and my instruments appear to be irretrievably lost. Habit, I suppose.

The pirates—some of them—appear to be preparing for a fresh voyage, leaving some of their band here to hunt for us. Meanwhile, we are still in hiding and have solved the cipher of the pine tree runes—but to our disappointment we find it tells us nothing. But digging further in the same spot we have found the true directions, which nearly stumped us:

STTSW MXIHM VIGXM SRWVI XYVRX SXVII KSXIR
TEGIW IEWXR MRIXC RSVXL JSVXC WSYXL
AIWXE RHHMK

It is not the cipher itself that stumped us—we deciphered the message easily and followed what it said—but we discovered nothing but soft sand! But then of course—how stupid of us not to have realized it at once—I realized it was not a simple cipher at all, but rather a combination of code and cipher—a form of nomenclator—with a clue in the first two words. Acting on that, we have at last located not only the two chests but also quantities of other booty. All of it together is too heavy to carry off, so we are now moving the treasure to another place—in haste, for the pirates still pursue us; we work at night while they camp and make merry. Half of our band are building rafts for our escape and the other half are hiding the treasure. Samuel is devising a way to record where it is hidden, disguising the instructions as a drawing of a pattern woven into fabric—dress goods for his sister. Clever lad!

A nomenclator—a secret message combining code and cipher—is a good way to stump—or nearly stump—experts like the Snows. What the pirates did first was to substitute code words for a couple of important words in their real message. They added a clue to the beginning of the real message—and then they put the whole thing, code words, clue, and all, into cipher.

The cipher the pirates used was a Caesar alphabet beginning with E—so it should be easy for you to decipher their message. When you have, see if you can figure out from the clue which words are in code, and what the code word substitutions are. (The answer is Number 6 on page 85.)

Most nomenclators are harder than the one the pirates used. They usually have more code words, for one thing. Here's one that's more like the usual kind:

1. *The Cipher:*
Half-and-Half Alphabet
A B C D E F G H I J K L M
N O P Q R S T U V W X Y Z

2. *The Code:*
Code Word Substitution

Real Word	Code Word
buried	lost
chests	ship's cat
left	sorrow
other	entire
pirate	ship's
booty	crew

3. *The Real Message:*
WE HAVE BURIED OUR CHESTS TO THE
LEFT OF THE OTHER PIRATE BOOTY

4. *How to Encipher:*
First, write out the real message, with the code words substituted for the real words:
WE HAVE LOST OUR SHIP'S CAT TO THE
SORROW OF THE ENTIRE SHIP'S CREW
Then put that already-disguised message into cipher. (Of course you'll lose the apostrophes, but that won't really matter in this case.)

JR UNIR YBFG BHE FUVCF PNG GB GUR
FBEEBJ BS GUR RAGVER FUVCF PERJ

Then divide that into five-letter "words" with a few harmless nulls:

JRUNI RYBFG BHEFU VCFPN GGBGU RFBEE
BJBSG URRAG VERFU VCFPE RJICA

And there you have a nomenclator message that will be hard to crack even if someone manages to figure out what cipher it's in!

To decode a nomenclator message like this, you need a list of the code words used. Without it, your job will be almost impossible. First, decipher the message. Then look up the code words—you may have to look up each word in the message—and put them back into their original form.

Try this one:

7. DEcipher and DEcode:

SVRHU REVUV VGGZO OCONJ

The cipher is Backwards Alphabet Cipher.
The code words are:

Code Word	Real Word
he	it
five	six
tall	left

(The answer is on page 86.)

Try making up your own nomenclators and using them with your friends. Remember to follow all three of these steps before you actually encode and encipher:

1. Write your real message out.

2. Make a list of its important words, and choose code words for them.

3. Choose your cipher.

Then go ahead: *first* encode and *then* encipher.

Answers for Chapter Six

1. To Mary for inform of period William Ann Diablo me valuable John Pace Setting Island as cargo Steere owner out period to if Flying of now Please nature possible Fish

To	Mary	for	inform	of	period
William	Ann	Diablo	me	valuable	John
Pace	Setting	Island	as	cargo	Steere
owner	out	period	to	if	Flying
of	now	Please	nature	possible	Fish

It's okay if you changed the capitalization when you encoded the message. In fact—congratulations if you did!

2. To Captain John Steere Flying Fish
Valuable cargo one chest jewels and one chest gold.
Also less important tobacco and ribbons.
Use great caution. Pace

Did you get that *dog* and *cat* were nulls? The real message was only 28 words long; two nulls were added to make six 5-word columns, 30 words in all:

To	Fish	jewels	period	and	caution
Captain	Valuable	and	Also	ribbons	period
John	cargo	one	less	period	Pace
Steere	one	chest	important	Use	dog
Flying	chest	gold	tobacco	great	cat

3. period From William Pace owner cargo valuable recover and rescue Set out at once to period crew strange with Island Has been glimpsed near Diablo period schooner pirate by captured Mary Ann missing and believed trader Coastal Fish Flying the To Captain John Steere Aboard

Somehow that one's a little too close to the real message for comfort! Maybe you can work out a better path.

4. The pirate schooner is sailing Thursday from Diablo Island. We would like everyone in the navy who is nearby to meet her at Diablo Island Bay. Plan for a big attack.

5. Sticking to the "Miss Blue" idea, you might come up with a message something like this:

Only two *good pitchers (navy ships)* are near
major league standard (Diablo Island).
They will leave immediately to *join (attack)*
the *Red Sox (pirate stronghold)*.

But you could have something really silly instead:

Only two *soapsuds (navy ships)* are near
gesundheit (Diablo Island). They will leave
immediately to *mollify (attack)* the *cheese
(pirate stronghold)*.

6. The real message, deciphered *and* decoded, is:
   OPPOSITE DIRECTIONS RETURN TO TREE
   GO TEN PACES WEST NINETY SOUTH FORTY
   NORTHEAST AND DIG

   Deciphered but *not* decoded, it reads:
   OPPOSITE DIRECTIONS RETURN TO TREE
   GO TEN PACES EAST NINETY NORTH
   FORTY SOUTHWEST AND DIG

   The clue to the code is in the words "opposite directions." This means that the true directions are *opposite*
   to those given. Since, then, directions opposite to those
   stated in the message are the real ones, *east* is really a
   code word for *west, north* is really a code word for
   south, and so on.

Of course a person could still be confused by the clue, because the word *directions* could mean *instructions,* not compass directions. Having a clue with two possible meanings may seem unfair—but to the encoders and those working with them, it's an added safeguard!

7. IT IS SIX FEET LEFT
Deciphered:
HE I S FIVE FEE T TALL X L M Q
S V R H U R E V U V V G G Z O O CON J

Decoded:
I T   S IX   LEFT
~~HE~~   I S   ~~FIVE~~   FEET   ~~TALL~~

7 | Hidden Codes and Ciphers

My dear Sister,

My travels being nearly over, I now turn my thoughts toward home and you and our dear mother, not to mention also a certain Young Lady living nearby, your close friend and, I hope, mine as well. To make up in some wise for being away so long, I wish to give both her and yourself some stuff for dresses, and I have crudely drawn the pattern of a fabric I propose to send or bring on my return; the drawing will I hope help you to begin the planning of such garments as you will make. The fabric I have in mind is two yards as it were easterly, and ten northerly, and here is the pattern, irregular, but I think pleasing:

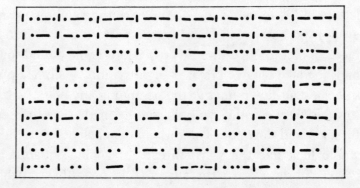

It is woven in several shades of blue and gray and very pretty, I think, though of course I am only a poor sailor and know little of such matters. If you do not like it, consider it is my poor drawing's fault, but if you consider that and like it not still, try to send word to me and I will find some other ladies for it.

Believe me, my dear Sister, I remain

Your loving Brother,
Sam

Sam's "poor drawing" is of course not of a piece of fabric at all, shades of blue and gray notwithstanding. Instead, it's a cleverly disguised secret message in, as you probably have guessed, Morse code. Morse isn't much good for really secret messages unless it is disguised, because so many people know it. But thinking up ways to disguise it can be fun.

To make his drawing, Sam first counted the number of letters in his message so he could set the symbols up in even rows that would look like the pattern woven into a piece of cloth. Since there were 76 letters, he added four nulls to make ten even rows of eight symbols each. He put short up-and-down lines at the beginning and end of each row and between the symbols, and he made sure to keep those up-and-down lines directly under each other so they would look like the warp threads of a piece of loosely woven fabric. (Warp threads are the ones that go this way: ↕ .) That meant that when he drew in the Morse symbols he had to vary the lengths of his dashes, and sometimes he had to put a single dot all by itself in the middle of a section—but since the message was fairly long, that wasn't the giveaway it could have been.

Can you decipher Sam's message—the all-important instructions for finding the pirate treasure—now that it's been hidden again? (The answer is Number 1 on page 105.)

This forest hides a message in two different ciphers, both of which you know. Can you figure out what the ciphers are and read the message? (The message is revealed in Number 2 on page 105.)

The next example of disguised secret writing can be done as either a cipher or a code. One of the people known for using it was Sir John Trevanion, who was put in prison in the seventeenth century for plotting against the English government. The story goes that he was sure he was about to be executed when a friend sent him a disguised coded message. To anyone reading it casually, the message seemed like an ordinary sympathetic letter—but luckily Sir John knew to ignore everything in it except the third letter after each punctuation mark. Reading it that way, he discovered there was a hidden escape route out of the prison chapel!

This same kind of disguised message was used by refugees during World War II. Many families were separated when they fled from their enemies in Europe. They could communicate only by letter—but of course a letter could easily fall into the wrong hands. So some clever people hid vital messages—like "Cross the border tomorrow"—in innocent-looking letters in which every third (or fourth, or whatever they decided on) word carried the meaning. The message "Cross the border tomorrow" might be hidden in a letter that read, "Mother is *cross*. She'll fix *the* trampled flower *border*, I think, *tomorrow*."

It's harder to write a message this way than it seems, for of course the secret message has to be hidden in a normal-sounding one—and it's not always easy to come up with a normal-sounding message that makes sense.

To use this hidden code, first write down your secret message, with lots of space between the words:

TO WILLIAM PACE
      PIRATES   SIGHTED
           IN   PURSUIT
    OF   TWO
SMALL   RAFTS   WE
    ATTACK   AT
    DAWN

                            John Steere

Then disguise the message by writing an innocent-sounding one around it. The hard part is arranging it so your secret message appears every third (or fourth, or whatever you decide) word—like this:

TO WILLIAM PACE
I KNOW PIRATES ARE SELDOM SIGHTED
HEREABOUTS OR IN PORT SO PURSUIT
IN PLACE OF SPYING WITH TWO OR THREE
SMALL BOATS OR RAFTS SUCH AS WE HAVE
INVITES ATTACK. WE ABANDON AT TOMORROW'S
EARLY DAWN OUR SEARCH.

John Steere

Although this "letter" doesn't read very smoothly once the secret message has been hidden in it, it's probably convincing enough to throw off all but the most suspicious of spies—and it does have the advantage of saying more or less the opposite of what the real secret message does.

Try these:

3. ENcode, hiding the secret message every third word:
POLE YOUR RAFT FASTER PIRATES ASTERN

4. DEcode: (You'll have to figure out if the message is hidden at every third word, or fourth word, or whatever.)

GREETINGS TO ONE AND ALL. MY
LONG TEDIOUS VOYAGE IS DONE. I
HAVE NOT LOST ANY MEN OR CARGO.
ONE BOAT LOOKS LIKE A RAFT,
HOWEVER, BATTERED AND BROKEN. IS
SMITH'S BOATSHOP, WHERE I'VE TAKEN
OTHER CRAFT, STILL OPERATING?

(The answers are on page 106.)

From the Charleston Gazette, *September 30:*

MONSTER STALKS SEAPORT
Residents
in
Fear

Charleston, Sept 29—Incredible though it seems, battle is being waged right here in our home port—battle waged by port authorities against a near monster calling himself El Diablo and claiming to rule an island in the Caribbean hard by major shipping and navy routes. Several men and women report being attacked on the docks, and small children have been tied mysteriously to an abandoned raft that appeared suddenly against one of the dock pilings.

The "monster" has been said to have unusually long teeth and heavy eyebrows; he wears a black cloak, a gold earring, and a red bandanna of the kind often sported by pirates. Police are on the alert but say the outcome of their attempts at arrest is uncertain as this creature operates unpredictably.

People are advised to stay away from the dock area at night, to send any word of sightings immediately to the police, and to call loudly for help at the slightest annoyance at the hands of any stranger in that area.

Hidden in that newspaper article is a secret message in one of the most wonderfully simple codes there is. All you have to do to send a message in Newspaper Code is take a page of a newspaper or, as in this case, a single newspaper article, and make a tiny dot—or better still, a pinprick—

under each word of your secret message, taking each word in order. You can send long messages quite safely this way, for it isn't at all unusual or suspicious-looking for one person to hand another a newspaper or to mail a newspaper clipping to a friend.

Can you read the message hidden in the *Gazette* article? (The answer is Number 5 on page 107.)

There are several possible variations on Newspaper Code. Instead of pricking out the words of your message, you can make it a cipher and prick out the letters instead. Just be sure you do it carefully—don't let your hand slip and hit the wrong letter. If you use letters instead of words, your message may have to be fairly short. But it may be easier to encipher, because you won't have to hunt through the paper for the right words in the right order.

You can make this code much harder—and much safer— if you first put your message into another code or cipher and then put pricks under the code words or cipher letters. That way if someone suspects you're using Newspaper Code and writes down the words or letters pricked, the resulting message won't make any sense.

Here's another disguise:

3	19	2	12
1	14	5	15
16	15	12	19
20	23	9	20
1		5	
9		22	
14		5	
		4	

Not too many people would think this was anything other than someone's arithmetic homework, but it's actually a cipher.

What's more, you can probably decipher it easily with just two pieces of information:

1. The cipher itself is Forwards Number Alphabet.

2. Each "example" is a word, to be read from top to bottom.

(And the answer is Number 6 on page 107.)

Here are some others to try:

7. ENcipher, in Backwards Number Cipher, disguised as arithmetic examples:

SAM SNOW TO THE RESCUE

8. DEcipher (you'll have to figure out which number cipher it's in):

16	3	1	19	6
9	1	14	14	9
18	16	4	15	7
1	20		23	8
20	1		19	20
5	9			9
	14			14
				7

8	20	8	9	23
1	15	1	14	1
14		14		20
4		4		5
				18

(The answers are on page 107.)

Here's a message in another disguised cipher:

```
01100    01000    10010    10000
00000    01110    01000    00000
10011    00101    01100    10010
10110    01000    00110    00100
10001    00110    01110    10001
00111    00111    01000
```

Looks like something you might get from a computer, doesn't it? But it's really a modern version of Bacon's old Aabab Cipher, which, as David Kahn points out in his excellent book *The Codebreakers* (Macmillan, 1967), converts well to a number system like that used in computer programming. Can you read the message? A = 0, B = 1, and the columns go from top to bottom. (The answer is Number 9 on page 108.)

Log entry   *John Steere*   Flying Fish

October 1   24° 15′N, 74° W

Hasting to Diablo Island this day, we came upon a great cloud of smoke obscuring the horizon. As we approached, we heard in the distance the sound of many cannons and the shouts of men in battle. This night we sailed closer, and there being a great haze of red in the air as from burning, we saw many men struggling and screaming in the water, several ship's boats and one raft having been smashed beyond repair and a navy ship sadly sinking. We took aboard as many men as we could, not attempting at the first to choose among pirate, merchant, or navy man, and we are even now not sure who is which. However, I grow sure of one prisoner—a gaunt and worn old man with a full beard, whose eyes are glassy with hunger and no doubt with horrors seen and suffered as well. He murmurs only what sounds like "sun" (or perhaps "son") and "gold," the latter making me think he must be the pirates' leader. Yet his manner is gentle and there are others among the survivors who insist he is Captain Joshua Snow. Therefore I think I must appear to believe them but still be wary of a scurvy pirate ruse intended to deceive me into befriending an impostor, in case he be such. The man will say no words save the mutterings I have recorded, as if his mind has somehow snapped—indeed, he has a great bruise on the side of his head, so that may well be so. Most of the time he does not even attempt to speak, but sits on deck idly writing random letters on paper, which he then hands to me with great ceremony, as if the letters spelled words of significance—but they are gibberish and only words in his poor mind, or words intended to deceive if impostor he be. A sample will suffice:

IVCLA RNZNU OATXS PPBED AAKYB MUZTN
MSUES LTOTJ EKLLL IYROT UWIMA PMLSV
NEOXW OATNE DUMFY LSGOQ NMAZN XDDMT
AUTME WALRQ ETAWD SRSIS FMTUO RNLAT
RAANF ZTETO HXEOC PASRV GFOHI MSHOJ
NTDWI AALBO LDOMM

It is sad to see what may be the destruction—if the man be Snow in truth—of what I know by reputation to have been a fine and active mind!

Of course if John Steere had known a little more about Captain Snow's reputation, or known him personally, he would have realized that any apparently random letters coming from Snow's pen were likely to be cipher—and if he had known something about cipher, he would have had even stronger suspicions, because he would have noticed that those "random" letters were neatly arranged in five-letter "words"!

Snow—for it was he—was using a cipher nicknamed "Swift's Swiftie," so called because it was used by English author Jonathan Swift and because it is very quick to encipher and decipher. At first glance, it looks like a substitution cipher. But it really isn't—it's a kind of transposition, because the letters of the real message are all there. In fact, they're even in their original order!

Look again at Snow's supposedly random scribbling. Copy the letters down one after the other, forgetting about the five-letter groupings. Then cross out (or erase) every other letter, starting with the second one. You should be left with this:

ICANNOTSPEAKBUTMUSTTELLYOUIAM
SNOWANDMYSONANDMATEAREADRIFT
ONARAFTTHECARGOISONDIABLOM

All you have to do now to read the message is correct the spacing. Look carefully along each line till you find words that make sense. (The message is completely deciphered in Number 10 on page 108.)

All you have to do to encipher a message in Swift's Swiftie is:

1. Write your message out in one long line, leaving spaces between the letters:

T H E R E I S N O F O O D O N T H E R A F T

2. Then fill in the spaces with any old letters you want, putting one letter in each space:

TAHLEQREE I S N O F O O D O N T H E R A F T

3. Finally, divide the result into five-letter "words":
TAHLE QRE . . .

In deciphering, if crossing out every other letter starting with the second letter doesn't work, try starting with the first!

Here are a couple to try:
11. ENcipher:
FIRST MATE FORTHER WOUNDED
12. DEcipher:
IQSLA VMPSR NZOMW QAMMZ TWROY PIBNC
GLTAO NKSET EZPXM MYDDL ICARR MYWBL
UPTQG ARTOS WNWSE YAJKI ELRKD ZAQIO
LPYLL
(The answers are on page 109.)

The next cipher—which can also be used as a code—looks like a number cipher but isn't. To use it, you and the receiver of your message must both have copies of the same edition of the same book. An ordinary school textbook is perfect, but we'll use this book for now, because that's the one we can be sure you have!

Here's what a message in that cipher—Book Cipher—looks like:

2 • 1 • 21   43 • 4 • 4   33 • 4 • 16   3 • 1 • 20   97 • 5 • 5
44 • 2 • 18   53 • 1 • 8   6 • 11 • 24   4 • 1 • 6   5 • 3 • 33
65 • 1 • 3   7 • 13 • 5   3 • 3 • 15   30 • 1 • 1   17 • 9 • 3
27 • 5 • 3   16 • 1 • 2   62 • 8 • 4   119 • 2 • 18

Each group of three numbers in Book Cipher stands for a single letter. The first number in each group stands for the *page* of the book on which the letter is found. The second stands for the *line* the letter is in on that page. And the third number stands for the *position* that letter is in within that line—3 if it's the third letter in the line, 25 if it's the twenty-fifth, and so on. The number 2 • 1 • 21, then, means you'll find the letter on page 2 in the first line—the twenty-first letter in that line. In this book, that's the letter T. (The answer is Number 13 on page 109.)

It's a good idea to skip around in your book when you're putting a message into this cipher, instead of just sticking to the first page or two. And it's also a good idea not to use pages in order. You can, for example, go from page 27 to page 3 to page 110 to page 18 even though you could probably find all the letters you need on a single page. It's safer to skip around because if the first number in every group were, say, 1, that would be a pretty good clue to anyone trying to crack your cipher.

Using this book:

14. ENcipher:

AT LAST CAUGHT A FISH FOR FOOD

(We can't tell you the answer to this one, because we have no way of knowing what pages you used!)

15. DEcipher:

2 · 1 · 23   2 · 1 · 9   53 · 3 · 1   29 · 1 · 18   19 · 1 · 1
133 · 2 · 1   13 · 4 · 17   4 · 2 · 9   89 · 1 · 30   62 · 24 · 8
81 · 1 · 14   42 · 2 · 11   43 · 1 · 13   6 · 3 · 2   88 · 1 · 9
62 · 3 · 21   75 · 12 · 13   79 · 2 · 9   127 · 19 · 6   94 · 2 · 5
96 · 10 · 16   44 · 1 · 2   4 · 1 · 10   67 · 12 · 11   48 · 1 · 29
48 · 2 · 32   50 · 1 · 9   20 · 1 · 1   75 · 7 · 1   5 · 5 · 6   5 · 1 · 9

(The answer is on page 110.)

The next cipher-in-disguise comes from one of the most famous detectives in the world, Sherlock Holmes. Holmes never lived, but that hasn't stopped millions of people from admiring and respecting him for nearly 100 years. He was the creation of Sir Arthur Conan Doyle, an English doctor-turned-writer who wrote many fascinating mysteries about Holmes and his best friend, Dr. Watson. In story after story, Holmes solves the most complicated of crimes using his amazing powers of observation and reasoning. A major clue in one crime Holmes solved was a cipher that looked, as Watson remarked, like "a child's drawing." Here is a message in the Cipher of the Dancing Men:

16.

And here is the cipher alphabet:

As you can see, the alphabet is incomplete—but you should still be able to decipher message Number 16. (The answer is on page 110.) The alphabet is incomplete because the messages Holmes deciphered in the story did not include the letters F, J, K, Q, U, W, X, and Z. Notice anything else wrong? If not, try writing

VAMPIRE

in Dancing Men Cipher. The "dancers" for V and P are the same. That was probably a typographical error made the first time the story was published (although some Sherlock Holmes experts think the mistake may have been deliberate on Conan Doyle's part and in some way part of the story). The same thing apparently happened to B and R too, but someone fixed that when the story was reprinted. You could finish correcting the cipher by making up a new dancer for V or P, and also by making up dancers for the missing letters. Then try enciphering this:

17. HAVE LOST TRACK OF TIME
    MATE PERHAPS DYING
    I AM WEAK
    SUN TOO HOT TO THINK
(The answer is on page 110.)

Log entry　　　*John Steere*　　　Flying Fish

October 8　　　　　　　　　*25°20′N, 74°10′W*
　I have moved us farther from the island. The weather is so hot and oppressive I fear a great windstorm of the kind

they often have at this time of year in these latitudes. I have therefore ordered all made secure and warned all hands of dirty weather to come. Several survivors of the pirate battle have died of their wounds and we have had some sad burials at sea. Oddly, there is little difference now between pirates and sailors—no conflict or rivalries, though we now know who is who. Wounds and hardship seem to have made all friends—that and lack of leadership among the pirates, for their captain, I am told, was killed in the battle by young Snow, who has disappeared.

Perhaps that is what agitates the old and speechless man, who, having gone from writing random letters to writing meaningless sums and lists of numbers separated with dots, has now taken to writing music. But when I asked my second mate, who has knowledge of the penny whistle and other simple instruments, to play one or two of the "songs" the old man has written, he told me they were tuneless—senseless jumbles of notes such as no musician would ever write. So I must put this down too to the snapping of the poor old man's mind. I am convinced now he must be Captain Snow, and it saddens me greatly to see him brought so low!

Snow's Song

No wonder the musical sailor couldn't get a tune out of this piece! It's not music—it's a cipher. Each note stands for a different letter of the alphabet—each KIND of note, regardless of where it is on the staff and what note it would be if it were played on the piano. For example, **d.** stands for the same letter—N—no matter where it appears. The rests (▬), which should always go on the second line from the top, separate the words of the message.

Here's the cipher alphabet:

A – d	H – #ℙ	O – ℙ.	V – #ℙ
B – #♩	I – #ℙ	P – ℙ.	W – bd
C – b♩	J – ℙ	Q – #d	X – bℙ
D – d	K – ℙ	R – bd	Y – #d.
E – d	L – ℙ	S – #ℙ	Z – bℙ.
F – d	M – d.	T – bℙ	
G – ℙ	N – d.	U – #d	

Can you read "Snow's Song" now? (The answer is Number 18 on page 110.)

In a way, the more you know about music the more convincingly you'll be able to use this cipher. But if you're a musician you've probably also already realized that there is a lot wrong with it musically! It would be almost impossible, for instance, to write a message correctly in, say, 4/4 time. For that reason, if you do know music, this cipher may make you angry! And non-musicians should realize that if a musician gets hold of a "song" in this cipher, he or she will certainly realize something's a little odd about it!

With those warnings, then, here are a couple for practice:

19. ENcipher:

ALL HANDS ON DECK

20. DEcipher:

(The answers are on page 111.)

Answers for Chapter Seven

1. FROM OLD OAK TO COAST THE ABOVE DISTANCES THEN TO ROUND BOULDER DIG WHERE THE RISING SUN HITS QVNL

    Look back in Sam's letter for "the above distances"—notice that he says the fabric is "two yards as it were easterly, and ten northerly"—seeming to give the dimensions a nautical flavor but in truth telling how far and in what direction toward the coast to go before digging!

2. Morse and runes are the ciphers. The message is:

    TREASURE HIDDEN RAFTS BUILT
    PIRATES PURSUING

1. The word TREASURE in Morse is hidden in the bark of the first tree on the left. The Morse symbols go down the trunk instead of from left to right, and the letters are separated by little slanting lines that have nothing to do with the message. Some of the dashes curve. The letters are arranged in order, in two columns.

2. The word HIDDEN is spelled out in runes by the first group of pine trees.

3. RAFTS is again in Morse.

4. BUILT is in runes.

5. PIRATES is in Morse.

6. PURSUING is in runes.

3. One possibility is:

NEAR NORTH POLE WE SAW YOUR SMALL WOODEN RAFT WE GO FASTER BUT NO PIRATES ARE CLOSE ASTERN

—but you're sure to have something quite different. It might be fun to see how many different cover messages you—or you and your friends—can come up with.

4. ALL IS LOST ONE RAFT IS TAKEN
The message is hidden at every fifth word:
GREETINGS TO ONE AND ALL. MY LONG TEDIOUS VOYAGE IS DONE. I HAVE NOT LOST ANY MEN OR CARGO. ONE BOAT LOOKS LIKE A RAFT, HOWEVER, BATTERED AND BROKEN. IS SMITH'S BOATSHOP, WHERE I'VE TAKEN OTHER CRAFT, STILL OPERATING?

5. INCREDIBLE BATTLE BEING WAGED NEAR
   DIABLO ISLAND BY MEN ON SMALL RAFT
   AGAINST PIRATES OUTCOME UNCERTAIN
   SEND HELP

6. CAPTAIN SNOW BELIEVED LOST
   In Forwards Number Alphabet, A = 1, B = 2, etc.
   So:

3	C	19	S	2	B	12	L
1	A	14	N	5	E	15	O
16	P	15	O	12	L	19	S
20	T	23	W	9	I	20	T
1	A			5	E		
9	I			22	V		
14	N			5	E		
				4	D		

7. Backwards Number Cipher: A = 26, B = 25, etc.

8	S	8	S	7	T	7	T	9	R
26	A	13	N	12	O	19	H	22	E
14	M	12	O			22	E	8	S
		4	W					24	C
								6	U
								22	E

8. PIRATE CAPTAIN AND SNOWS FIGHTING
   HAND TO HAND IN WATER

The message is in Forwards Number Cipher: A = 1, B = 2, etc.

16	P	3	C	1	A	19	S	6	F
9	I	1	A	14	N	14	N	9	I
18	R	16	P	4	D	15	O	7	G
1	A	20	T			23	W	8	H
20	T	1	A			19	S	20	T
5	E	9	I					9	I
		14	N					14	N
								7	G

8	H	20	T	8	H	9	I	23	W
1	A	15	O	1	A	14	N	1	A
14	N			14	N			20	T
4	D			4	D			5	E
								18	R

9. NAVY SHIP FIGHTING PIRATES

01100 = abbaa = N 00101 = aabab = F 01110 = abbba = P
00000 = aaaaa = A 01000 = abaaa = I 01000 = abaaa = I
10011 = baabb = V 00110 = aabba = G 10000 = baaaa = R
10110 = babba = Y 00111 = aabbb = H 00000 = aaaaa = A
10001 = baaab = S 10010 = baaba = T 10010 = baaba = T
00111 = aabbb = H 01000 = abaaa = I 00100 = aabaa = E
01000 = abaaa = I 01100 = abbaa = N 10001 = baaab = S
01110 = abbba = P 00110 = aabba = G

10. I CANNOT SPEAK BUT MUST TELL YOU I AM SNOW AND MY SON AND MATE ARE ADRIFT ON A RAFT THE CARGO IS ON DIABLO

ICANNOTSPEAKBUTMUSTTELLYOU
IAMSNOWANDMYSONANDMATEARE
ADRIFTONARAFTTHECARGOISON
DIABLOM

11. FᴬIᴸR ˢSᴿTQ MᴾABT CEDFM OᴿRᴼT
    ˢHᴾET RQWᶻO WUᴸNᶻ DMEᴾD

Your answer will be different—you will have different letters where the handwritten ones are. That's fine—just so you still have all the regular letters in this order and in these positions.

12. I SAM SNOW AM TRYING TO KEEP MY
    DIARY BUT GROW WEAKER DAILY

Cross out every other letter starting with the second:

IØSᴸA ᴶMᴾSᴷ NᶻOᴹW ØAᴹMᶻ
TᴶRØY ᴶIᴮNᶜ GᴸTᴬO ᴶKᴶEᴶ
EᶻPᴶM ᴶYØDᴸ IᶜAᴷR ᴶYWBᴸ
UᴾTØG ᴶRᴶOᴶ WᴶWᴶE ᴶAᴶKᴶ
EᴸRᴷD ᶻAØIØ LᴶYᴸL

Write down the letters that are left, and find the words:

ISAM**SNOW**AM**TRYING**TO**KEEP**MY
DIARYBUTGROW**WEAKER**DAIL**YL

13. THIRD DAY OUT MATE WEAK

T	H	I	R	D	D	A
2·1·21	43·4·4	33·4·16	3·1·20	97·5·5	44·2·18	53·1·8

Y	O	U	T	M	A	T
6·11·24	4·1·6	5·3·33	65·1·3	7·13·5	3·3·15	30·1·1

E	W	E	A	K
17·9·3	27·5·3	16·1·2	62·8·4	119·2·18

14. No answer possible.

15. HOT AND DRY NO RAIN FOR
DRINKING WATER

H	O	T	A	N	D	D
2·1·23	2·1·9	53·3·1	29·1·18	19·1·1	133·2·1	13·4·17

R	Y	N	O	R	A	I
4·2·9	89·1·30	62·24·8	81·1·14	42·2·11	43·1·13	6·3·2

N	F	O	R	D	R	I
88·1·9	62·3·21	75·12·13	79·2·9	127·19·6	94·2·5	96·10·16

N	K	I	N	G	W	A
44·1·2	4·1·10	67·12·11	48·1·29	48·2·32	50·1·9	20·1·1

T	E	R
75·7·1	5·5·6	5·1·9

16. MOONLIGHT VERY COLD THIRSTY

Did you notice the little flags some of the dancers are
holding? They separate words.

17. You'll need some new dancers for this one. Here
are the ones we used, but yours can be different.
(We decided to keep the original dancer for P and
change V.)

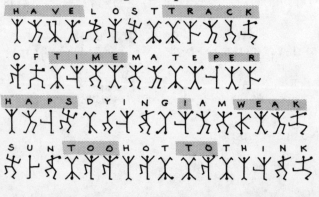

Here is the message, enciphered:

18. MY SON IS ADRIFT PLEASE SEARCH

Remember not to pay any attention to where the
notes are on the staff. In fact, you can copy them
down next to each other, without the staff, and then
decipher the message:

19.

You're sure to have your notes in other positions on
the staff. That's fine—the important thing is that you
have the right *kinds* of notes. Where you place them
isn't important for the cipher.

20. STRIKE ALL SAIL THE STORM COMES

8 | Code and Cipher Machines You Can Find or Make

A code or cipher "machine" is any mechanical object that helps you write or solve a code or cipher. It can be as simple as a telephone or as complicated as a computer. There are several machines—like the telephone—that you can find around the house, and there are also several that you can make out of simple, everyday materials.

Let's start with the telephone.

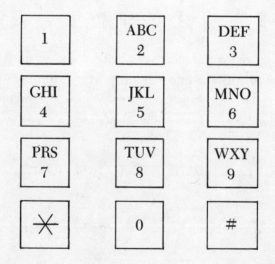

This is a push-button phone, but you can use a regular dial phone (although you may have to make a few minor changes).

To use a phone as a cipher machine, you have to work out a system that will give you substitutions for the letters of the alphabet. There are several possible ways to do this. One of the best is to make up a number substitution cipher using group and position numbers based on a checkerboard—the way you did with runes. For the group numbers, use the numbers on the push buttons. For the position numbers, use 1, 2, or 3, depending on whether the letter you want is the first, second, or third one on the button. (You'll have to work out something special for Q and Z if you need them, for, as you can see, they aren't on the phone.) In this system, A would be 2 • 1, B would be 2 • 2, N would be 6 • 2, and so on.

Try deciphering this:

```
4•2  8•2  7•2  7•2  4•3  2•3  2•1  6•2
3•2  9•1  2•1  7•2  6•2  4•3  6•2  4•1
7•3  7•1  6•3  7•3  8•1  3•2  3•1
```

(The answer is Number 1 on page 135.)

Here's the same message in another Phone Cipher, also using a push-button phone. Can you figure out the system used?

```
7•2  0•2  *•2  *•2  7•3  5•3  5•1  9•2
6•2  #•1  5•1  *•2  9•2  7•3  9•2  7•1
      *•3  *•1  9•3  *•3  0•1  6•2  6•1
```

(The system is described in Number 2 on page 135.)

Look around your house or apartment for other common objects you could use for cipher machines. Anything with numbers usually has possibilities—clocks, for example, and radio dials. How about the dial on the oven? Or the numbers and lines on an outside thermometer? Or a typewriter keyboard?

This next machine, as Captain Snow realized, dates from ancient Greece.

Log entry   John Steere   *Flying Fish*

October 9
The storm has been fierce and still blows around us, though there is now a sudden lull. But there is no sun or star by which to fix our position. We are, however, still not far from Diablo Island, unless I miss my guess. So far we have survived well, though under bare poles. I fear this is one of those storms that blows with renewed fury after just such a lull as we are having now.

During its height some time before the lull, the storm blew us an odd passenger: a large gull, sodden, exhausted, with fastened to its leg a strip of even more sodden paper, covered with tiny marks. We unrolled the strip but could make nothing of it till one of the men produced a glass that makes things appear larger—and then, on the unrolled strip, we saw this:

```
O
N  B  N
N  D  A  O
R  I  Y  W
A  A  S
F  B  A
T  L  M
I  O  S
```

    Although obviously the writing must be the work of a human being, no human here could make sense of it. But then the old man seized the gull with an odd cry. He took the paper strip from my hand, rolled it again around the bird's leg—and then, with the aid of the glass, gently turning the bird so we could read it all, we saw:

The old man then seized paper and, writing frantically, told me by ordinary writing and much to my astonishment that he is indeed Captain Snow, that his injuries were such that at first he could barely speak (and still cannot), and that he found he could write only in the ciphers he had· studied for years—not in plain English. This cipher of the bird—ancient Greek scytale, he called it—jolted some injured part of his brain, allowing him suddenly to think and write in plain English instead of cipher, praises be! And therefore now he writes us both his needs and his story, for still he cannot speak—at least not much or clearly. Indeed I have heard of such marvelous strange injuries, where some single faculty is lost while others yet remain, but never until now have I witnessed it.

The wind is freshening; I must go above. When the storm abates we shall of course begin our search for Captain Snow's son Samuel—though I fear in such a gale no man could long survive on a mere simple raft.

Impossible as Captain Snow's injuries may seem, the cipher he took from the gull's leg is not impossible at all. Scytale is thought to have been used in ancient Greece and uses a simple and effective cipher machine you can make easily—it is just a plain cylinder. To send a message using a scytale, you will need:

2 scytales—identical cylinders—one for you, one for your partner. (Paper towel rolls are good. You can also use pencils if you don't mind writing small!)
transparent tape
pencil
plain paper
scissors

Cut your paper into long strips. You are going to write the letters of your message on the strips *after* you wrap the strips around one of the cylinders. For a short message, you'll probably need only one strip, but for a long one, you might have to fasten two or three together with tape.

Now wrap your paper strip around the cylinder. Start by fastening the end of the strip to the cylinder with tape. Do *not* let the edges of the strip overlap! To prevent that, you may have to start your wrapping on a slight angle— like this:

Tape

Continue to wrap on an angle, and leave a little space after each section of the strip as it comes around the cylinder again:

When you reach the end of the strip, fasten it lightly to the cylinder with tape. Then write your message in the ordinary way from left to right across the cylinder. Put only *one* letter on each section of strip—like this.

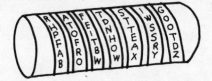

The message shown above is RAFT SIGHTED TWO POINTS OFF THE STARBOARD BOW. Note the nulls at the end. How long a message you can write will depend on the size of your cylinder and how long your strip is. Your message can, of course, go all the way around the cylinder, not just partway as shown here.

Now all you have to do to send this message is unroll the paper strip—which will then look like this:

—and send it to your partner. The message won't look like much of anything if it falls into the wrong hands, but all your partner has to do to read it is wrap the paper strip carefully around his or her scytale and the message will appear again in rows from left to right.

Here's a message enciphered with another machine that's very easy to make:

TO ALL U. S. NAVAL SHIPS IN AREA OF DIABLO BAY:

S M Z A M P S R N T O L Z W F

P I Q C B K L Z E D T R U Y X

P W O W Z N A D R E A F G H T

S S A T R Y S Q C L A R O G M

O O N Y N T S I S Q L A B N H

D J A L I L L S H I M P R S Z

G S O I T O K I O S P L Z A F

N M D R I M L M E Z D I F A Z

T P E Q L L Y T

The machine used for enciphering that message is called a Cardano grille. It was named after the sixteenth-century Italian doctor Girolamo Cardano, who wrote many books about science and included cryptology (the study of secret writing) in two of them.

A message enciphered with the aid of a Cardano grille must be deciphered with the aid of an identical grille, just the way a message sent in scytale must be enciphered and deciphered with scytales of identical sizes. Here's a picture of the Cardano grille used for the message to the naval ships:

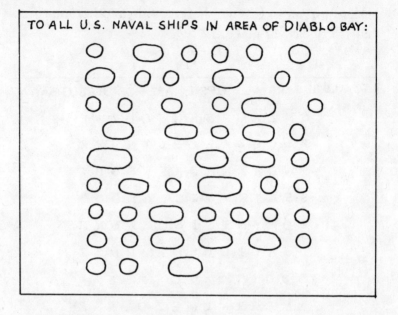

To read the message above, first trace the drawing of the grille onto the heaviest paper you can see through. Then carefully cut out each of the little circles. Put your grille on top of the enciphered message and read the real message through the holes. (See Number 3 on page 136 if your grille didn't work.)

To make Cardano grilles of your own, you will need:

2 pieces of lightweight cardboard (shirt cardboard
  or the cardboard from the backs of pads of paper)
scissors (nail scissors are good)
pencil
paper

Let's say your secret message is:

SAM IS SAFE

You can probably remember this message easily, but if you have a long one, jot it down on a scrap of paper so you won't forget it as you make your grille. To make the grille, write the message in large letters on a piece of cardboard. Space it irregularly, perhaps like this:

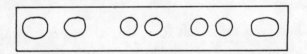

(For a longer message use several lines—but keep the letters in the right order.)

Cut the letters out very carefully so there is a little hole in the cardboard where each letter was. For letters that are right next to each other, like SA, just cut one hole, but always be careful to make the holes as close to the size of the letters as you can. Throw the letters away when you've cut them out!

Now you have a Cardano grille for this message. It should look something like this:

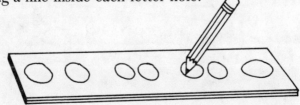

Make an identical grille for your partner by putting your grille on top of the other piece of cardboard and drawing a line inside each letter hole:

Then cut out the holes.

Be very careful not to slip when you're drawing or cutting. If your partner's grille isn't *exactly* the same as yours, he or she won't be able to read your message!

To encipher your message, put one of the grilles on top of a piece of paper and write the message through the holes:

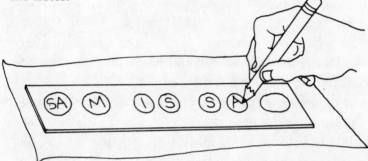

Then remove the grille and fill in the spaces between the letters with any old additional letters, like this:

A Q S A L I M Z Y I L S P T O L S J A P I F E

And there you are! That long line of letters is your enciphered message. To decipher it, all your friend has to do is hold his or her Cardano grille over the paper and read the message through the holes.

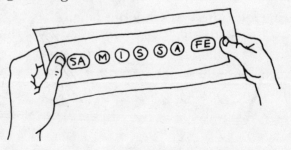

Warning! Make sure you throw away the first piece of paper—the one you wrote your message on if it was a long one.

And even though you'll need a new grille for each new message, be careful not to leave grilles lying around where some unauthorized person might find them.

You can also use a Cardano grille to send a coded message. For this, you and your friend need identical copies of the same edition of the same book—or magazine or newspaper. Find a page or a section of a page that contains all the words in your real message (you may have to rewrite your real message a little to get the same words). Then put a thin piece of paper over the page and draw a close-fitting circle around each word you want. Fasten the paper to a piece of cardboard and cut through both paper and cardboard to make the first grille.

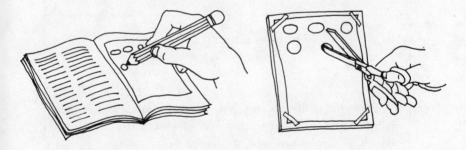

Make the second grille the same way you did the first.

Instead of fastening the paper to the cardboard and cutting through both, you could draw your holes and then put the paper on top of the cardboard and draw around the holes again, this time with a blunt pencil—the pencil

may make enough of a mark on the cardboard to serve
as a guide for cutting. Or put a piece of carbon paper between the paper and the cardboard, and draw around the
holes again. (Make sure you have the carbon paper shiny
side down.)

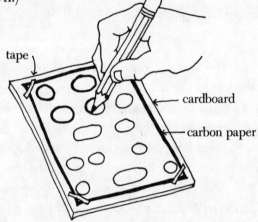

tape

cardboard

carbon paper

Log Entry by Captain Joshua Snow,
aboard the Flying Fish

October 15. 24° 15′N, 74° W

Though this be not my own ship, I cannot break the
habit of stating our position and of giving the weather,
which be fair at last with a good steady east wind and a
smoothly rolling sea. Those who speak of the calm before
the storm would do well also to speak of the calm—at least
the peace—that often follows it.

I have now revealed to Captain Steere that much of my
illness except at the beginning was feigned. I have also
told him that the reason for my deception was that the

pirate captain's first mate was aboard as prisoner on this ship and his intentions towards me were evil and murderous—for he was aware I had found and rehidden the cargo. It was clear his plan was to force the cargo's location out of me and then murder me—but as long as I could not speak or write in any way that made sense to him (it was only the pirate captain, I believe, who knew cipher)—as long as I made no sense to the pirate mate, I was safe. I therefore feigned to "speak" in cipher, thinking that might give him hope of my "recovery" and also perhaps enable me to communicate with Captain Steere. That last was not to be; Steere knows not cipher.

The best news of all, which I have saved to savor, is that my beloved son Samuel is safe! The storm blew us one good thing—nay, two, for it blew us first the gull with the news of him and then him himself, after the storm had abated and the navy had arrived and taken off its own men, and also the pirates as prisoners. Alas, I weep for my poor first mate Forther, who, Sam told me, drowned in the storm despite Sam's efforts to save him. But destroyed as I am with weeping for my noble, good mate, whom I shall sorely miss, I at the same time rejoice and give thanks that my son; my beloved son, is safely restored to me and to his mother and sister.

And now it pleases me to set down in this log that we sail back to Diablo Island once more, this time, if luck be with us, at last to recover the cargo and my beloved ship, which I shall be glad to return after all to its owner, William Pace; to recover the other booty the pirates hid; and also, happily, to find and free the poor wretches whom we had to leave behind in the pirate dungeon. Truly, but for the loss of my mate, my heart could be as merry as the sun that now shines so bravely upon the sparkling sea!

Hidden in Captain Snow's log entry is a message using this Cardano grille:

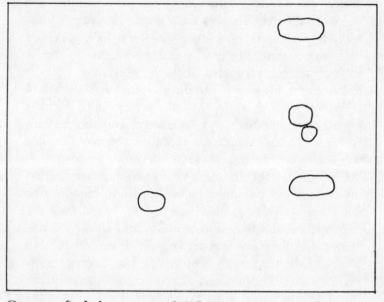

Can you find the message? (The answer is Number 4 on page 137.)

(The answer is Number 4 on page 137.)

From the Charleston Gazette, *October 30*
MARY ANN, CARGO
R E C O V E R E D !
Miraculous Rescue!

Charleston, Oct. 29—Incredible as it will seem to our readers, the missing coastal trader *Mary Ann* sailed into port today, carrying not only her captain, Joshua Snow, and most of her crew, but also Snow's son Samuel, missing from *The Pride of Charleston* for many months, plus a number of that good ship's crew as well. And as if that were not miracle enough, the *Mary Ann* also bore home much of her original cargo—intact!

"One or two bales of ribbons are missing," said owner William Pace, "not to mention all the tobacco she was carrying, but the important cargo—two chests of valuables—has been fully recovered, thanks to the ingenuity of Snow and his son."

Mr. Pace, along with the Snows and Captain John Steere of the *Flying Fish,* who assisted in the dramatic rescue, then told an amazing tale of piracy on the high seas. Much of the story must be saved for the trial of the pirates, many of whom were captured in a battle that raged for nearly two days in the bay off Diablo Island. However, a few facts emerged and may be stated: that young Snow had been kept prisoner aboard the pirate ship for some time; that the self-same pirate captain captured the *Mary Ann* and her cargo; that both Snows and numerous crew members were imprisoned for a time on Diablo Island, where were also the bulk of the prisoners from *The Pride of Charleston;* that the valuable cargo from the *Mary Ann* was hidden there—and that the Snows, using a combination of wit, courage, and daring, not only escaped from their dungeon, but somehow also found the *Mary Ann*'s cargo and rehid it from the pirates since they could not carry it away.

"The Snows used cipher to write down where they hid it," Captain Steere told the *Gazette,* clearly filled with admiration for the two men. "And to find out where the pirates had hidden it in the first place, they had to read cipher. Turns out they're experts in that field, both of them—along with being courageous and loyal. William Pace owes them a lot for getting that cargo back, not to mention the ship too, of course."

The trial of the pirates is set for Tuesday next, right here in Charleston. It is sure to reveal even more amazing details of this truly amazing sea tale!

Found on the same page of the Gazette, *deep in the bottom right-hand corner:*

> Captain st. cyr:
> UCQOP JVYGC JYLXL
> OPJZU KWIUK YZCKC
> QOPKJ YLOLQ CEBYO
> PYUPJ LIJVB YGCLY
> UGURR BYCJE OILJL
> UCRDE
>
> First Mate Barton

How handy that the name of the pirate captain was St. Cyr—for St. Cyr is also a famous machine cipher, named after a French military academy where it was frequently used in the late 1800s.

To make a St. Cyr cipher machine and decipher the message hidden in the *Gazette*, you will need:

graph paper   pen
lightweight cardboard scissors
ruler   tape or glue

A finished St. Cyr machine looks like this:

To make your St. Cyr machine, cut a piece of cardboard so that it measures about 2 inches by 6½ inches. Cut a piece of graph paper the same size. Leaving margins of about ¾ inch on each side, write an alphabet—one letter per square—towards the top of the graph paper. Label it *Real Alphabet:*

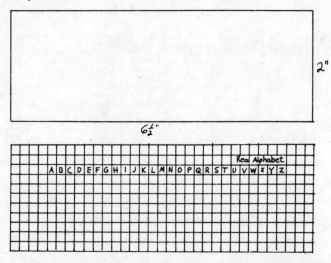

Then glue or tape the graph paper to the cardboard.

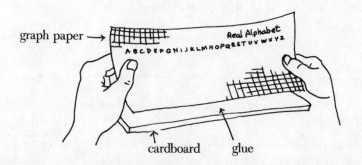

Now cut a strip of cardboard about 11 inches long and ¾ of an inch wide. Cut a strip of graph paper the same size.

Write two backwards alphabets on the graph paper (again, one letter per square) and label them *Cipher and Key:*

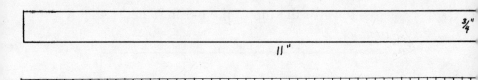

Tape or glue the paper strip to the cardboard strip. (If you'd rather, you can make the machine out of graph paper alone—or plain paper—but it will be much stronger if you use cardboard, and easier to line up if you use graph paper, as you'll see.)

Now draw a line a little below the outside edge of the A of the real alphabet on the larger piece of cardboard, and another line a little below the outside edge of the Z (see drawing). The lines should be just a little bit longer than the width of the thin strip of cardboard—about ¾ inch up and down.

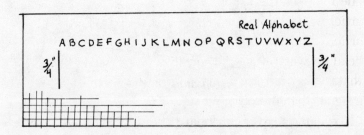

Cut carefully along the lines to form a slot at each, and poke the thin strip of cardboard (the one marked *Cipher and Key) up* through one slot and *down* through the other.

The backwards alphabets on the thin strip should now be below the frontwards alphabet on the larger piece of cardboard:

And now you have a St. Cyr machine.

You can use this machine in a number of ways. A good one involves the use of a *key letter.* In the short *Gazette* article, the clue to the key letter was in the heading of the article. Did you notice that the only capital letter in the heading was the C in Captain? That was really a signal that the key letter was C. The name St. Cyr, of course, was a signal that the cipher used was the St. Cyr Cipher.

To decipher the message, you'll have to set your machine—that's what the key letter is for. Move your long strip of cardboard along till its first C is underneath the A of the real alphabet:

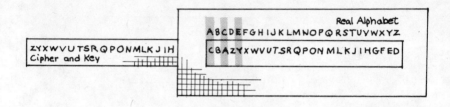

Now your machine is set. Remember that the cipher alphabet is the one on the narrow strip; the real alphabet is the one above it. Notice that A in the real alphabet is C in the cipher alphabet. B in the real alphabet is B in the cipher alphabet. C in the real alphabet is A in the cipher alphabet. D in the real alphabet is Z in the cipher alphabet. And so on.

You should now be able to decipher the message in the *Gazette*. (See Number 5 on page 137 if you have trouble.)

You can get many different cipher alphabets from this simple machine. To get a new one, simply choose a new key letter and move the narrow strip till that letter appears under the real letter A.

In St. Cyr Cipher, using your machine:

6. ENcipher, with the key letter R:
   ORDER IN THE COURT

7. DEcipher, with the key letter L:
   SELSZ LYDTL SULDS XUPON

(The answers are on page 137.)

From the Charleston Gazette, *November 4*
DRAMA IN COURT
"Monster" Appears
PIRATES SENTENCED

Charleston, Nov. 3—Never in this reporter's memory has there been such a trial as that in progress at our very own Charleston Courthouse for the past few days!

First the men of the *Mary Ann* and of *The Pride of Charleston* telling their sad tale of brutal treatment at the hands of the pirate St. Cyr and his men. Then the tale of the "valuable cargo"—revealed as precious jewels and gold—told by William Pace, owner of the *Mary Ann.* The battle—the rescue in a mammoth storm—the recovery of the treasure—all these events are as well known by now to our readers as is the guilty verdict pronounced yesterday by the foreman of the jury in righteous ringing tones.

But none of this can be topped by today's events when, principals and spectators having gathered to hear the judge pronounce sentence, there slithered into the courtroom a disreputable figure, bearded, clothed in black save for a pirate's bandanna, snarling, and baring his teeth. His eyes darted madly around the room as he demanded to see Captain St. Cyr—who of course was killed in the battle—and then, not seeing him, the Monster of the Waterfront—for it was he—sank sobbing onto the floor!

It at last emerged after lengthy testimony that this man was once St. Cyr's first mate, one Barton by name, and, betrayed in some matter between pirates, he deserted the *Barbary Scourge* when she was last near Charleston. He then set himself up on the waterfront here, by day venging himself on St. Cyr, his former captain, by warning those embarking on voyages that pirates plied the coast.

Samuel Snow, who witnessed his desertion and heard his plan, sent a warning by him when he himself was being held prisoner.

By night, First Mate Barton terrorized the residents of Charleston in his now notorious "monster" garb—"To get money to live on," he whined to the judge, but to his victims it must seem more because he is at heart a pirate still and must therefore live by terror.

And so at last the Monster of the Waterfront was led away, to be tried later for his alleged assaults on the good people of Charleston, and the matter of sentencing his former shipmates went forward. The spectators applauded as the judge pronounced sentence one by one upon the pirates according to their individual crimes, with great fairness.

Tonight, we are told, the officers and crews of the *Mary Ann* and of *The Pride of Charleston* and of the *Flying Fish* plan a gala party, at which it is said that Captain Snow will demonstrate some of his amazing knowledge of secret writing. And we of the *Gazette* offer a prize to anyone who can solve this puzzle Captain Snow delivered us this morning: TA TSAL EHT ETARIP EGRUOCS SI DEDNE.

The answer is Number 8 on page 137. If you got it, congratulations! It's very hard to solve a cipher when you don't have any clues to what the cipher is. In the next chapter, along with new, nonpirate messages to solve, you'll find pointers about how to do that. Meanwhile, so you won't be *on the fence,* as the saying goes, for long, here's another message (once you find the clue, the message should be easy to decipher):

IOEOV HDSUH URAIG HSOKS VHDRT NIGOL
CITEA THPEX HPYUE AAMCF NEDNT IBOAI
EAWII GTODU KNHLS CATRY

(The message is deciphered in Number 9 on page 138.)

Answers for Chapter Eight

1. HURRICANE WARNINGS POSTED

H	U	R	R	I	C	A	N	E
4·2	8·2	7·2	7·2	4·3	2·3	2·1	6·2	3·2

W	A	R	N	I	N	G	S
9·1	2·1	7·2	6·2	4·3	6·2	4·1	7·3

P	O	S	T	E	D
7·1	6·3	7·3	8·1	3·2	3·1

2. This is based on the same basic idea, *except* each group number is from the button *below* the one the letter is on, instead of from the same button. A, B, and C, then, are in Group 5 in this cipher, instead of in Group 2 (A is 5 · 1, B is 5 · 2, C is 5 · 3). M, N, and O are in Group 9 instead of in Group 6, and W, X, and Y are in Group #.

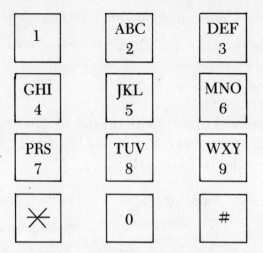

If you have the round kind of dial on your phone, you could try inventing a similar cipher by using the numbers on, before, or after the letter groups you want.

3. SAM SNOW PICKED UP ON RAFT
   SAYS CARGO ON ISLAND ALL SHIPS
   GO TO ISLAND IMMEDIATELY

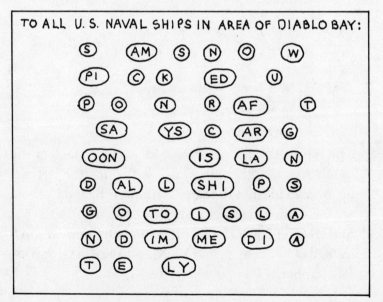

4. DESTROY LOG IF PIRATES FIND

(The message starts in line 8 in paragraph three of the log entry.)

5. I AM ON THE WATERFRONT DISGUISED
AS A MONSTER OR MAYBE ONE IN TRUTH
BEWARE I WILL BE AT YOUR TRIAL <u>ZY</u>

The machine set up correctly looks like this:

6. DAONA JEYKN PDXAY

7. THAT MAN IS A TRAITOR <u>WXY</u>

8. AT LAST THE PIRATE SCOURGE HAS
ENDED

The cipher is Backwards Word Cipher.

9. This is in Rail Fence Cipher, as you probably guessed from the words "on the fence." Put back into its Rail Fence form it looks like this:

I O E O V H D S U H U R A I G HS
 H P Y U E A A M C F N E D N T I

O K S V H D R T N I G O L C I
B O A I E A W I I GT O D U KN

T E A T H P E X̲
 H L S C A T R Y̲

Deciphered, it reads:
I HOPE YOUVE HAD AS MUCH FUN READING
THIS BOOK AS IVE HAD WRITING IT GOOD
LUCK IN THE LAST CHAPTER
(Apologies for the loss of the apostrophes!)

9 | Messages to Solve— and How to Solve Them

Note: The first part of this chapter is pretty hard, but it will help you solve ciphers for which you don't have any clues. But don't worry—there *are* clues for the harder ciphers in the "Messages to Solve" section of this chapter.

Up to now, you've been reading this book from the point of view of someone who is sending secret messages or receiving them from a friendly partner. Now imagine yourself as a spy who has just seized what appears to be an important communication from the enemy. Only trouble is, it looks like this:

REHPI CAGNI VLOST HGINL LAPUY ATSNA CUOYX

It's pretty obvious that the message is in cipher—but how do you tell which one?

The first thing you have to decide is whether it's in a transposition cipher or a substition cipher. One way to do that is to count the number of vowels (A, E, I, O, U). If the message has a lot of vowels in it, you can be pretty sure it is a transposition cipher. Just about every word in English contains at least one vowel—and you know that in a transposition cipher you have all the real letters right in front of you. That means in any transposition cipher you're going to see a fair number of vowels. In the message above, there are 12 vowels. The chances are excellent, then, that it's in a transposition cipher.

But even though the chances are good, you can't be 100 percent certain. As long as there are clever cryptographers whose job it is to invent indecipherable ciphers, there will be plenty of ciphers that seem to be what they aren't.

The next step, when you think a message is in a transposition cipher, is to figure out if it's in either Backwards Word Cipher or Backwards Message Cipher, because they're the two easiest transposition ciphers to spot. Then if that doesn't work, try the other transposition ciphers you've learned. You can test for simple Rail Fence quite easily by trying out the shortcut deciphering method you read about in Chapter Two. Twisted Paths Cipher, though, will be a lot harder both to recognize and to decipher. In fact, all but the simplest transposition ciphers are harder to solve than most substitution ciphers because there are so very many ways in which the letters of a message can be rearranged.

Have you figured out the message yet? It's deciphered under A on page 155.

Although substitution ciphers are often easier to solve, that doesn't mean that they're *all* easy or that solving them doesn't take a lot of time. Ones that use special symbols—Pigpen, Dancing Men—are easy to spot, but those that use letters, numbers, or symbols you've never seen before are much harder. The most important thing to do when you are faced with a substitution cipher you don't recognize is to count how many times each letter or symbol has been used. If you find a lot of X's in a message, for example, there's a good chance that X stands for E, because E is the most frequently used letter in English. (It might be T, A, or O, too, as you'll see in a minute.) Another important thing to look for—if the message hasn't been divided into fake "words"—is one-letter words. (There are only three possible ones: A, I, and O.) Then—again, if the message isn't in fake "words"—look for double letters, for two- and three-letter words (OF, TO; THE, AND), and for pattern words —words in which one or more letters have been repeated. Then try out the possibilities you've found. For example— keeping in mind that THE is a very common three-letter word—if you have a word that looks like this in a cipher message:

&5@

try writing a T every time you see the symbol & through- out the entire message, an H every time you see 5, and an E every time you see @. Combine that with letters you're trying out for one- and two-letter words and for pattern words and see if anything begins to make sense. If not, try other common possibilites. It's a little like doing a crossword puzzle.

Here are some general rules about English that should help you solve substitution ciphers:

1. The most common letter is E. After that come T, A, O, N, R, I, S, H, and D, in that order.

2. The *only* one-letter words are A, I, and once in a great while, O. A appears much more often than I. (Initials, of course, can be single letters—or things like X in X marks the spot—so be a little careful of this!)

3. Common double letters are SS, EE, TT, FF, LL, MM, and OO.

4. The most common two-letter words are OF, TO, IN, IT, and IS.

5. The most common three-letter word is THE, and the next most common is AND.

6. The most common four-letter word is THAT. It's a pattern word: It begins and ends with the same letter—the common letter T.

7. T is very common as the first letter of words. It is also common as the last.

8. E is the most common last letter.

9. N often comes right after a vowel.

10. There is *always* a U after a Q.

11. V, K, X, J, Q, and Z are the *least* common letters in English.

You can find these and other rules (often under the heading "Frequency Tables") in many good books about cipher—check the list in the back of this book for a few.

Okay—now try this:

LQJYCNA WRWN VNBBJPNB CX BXUEN

This message looks like a substitution cipher, because it contains very few vowels. Luckily it doesn't seem to have been divided into fake "words." Let's try using some of the rules above to solve it:

1. There are 5 N's and 4 B's—so it's possible that they might stand for E and T (see Rule 1).

2. There is one two-letter word (see Rule 4).

3. There are two pattern words, one with two W's and the other with:

    a) a double letter: BB in the cipher,

    b) a repeated letter: N in the cipher,

    c) an additional B.

(No specific rule applies, but it's easier to fill in the "blanks" in a pattern word than in other words: _IGH_, for example, could be <u>T</u>IGH<u>T</u> or <u>S</u>IGH<u>S</u>.)

You could go ahead now and try to solve this message, using whatever rules seem to fit—and you might be successful. But some cipher experts would suggest that before you do that, you check for one of the most common substitution ciphers: a Caesar alphabet.

To do that, you have to try each of the 25 possible Caesar alphabets. That could take a long time! Luckily there's a shortcut: your St. Cyr machine. Instead of writing out all the Caesar alphabets, just make a Caesar strip for your St. Cyr machine by writing two *forwards* alphabets on a narrow strip of graph paper and pasting it on a strip of cardboard, to make it extra strong. (Label your Caesar strip so you won't mix it up with your St. Cyr one!) By sliding this strip along under the real alphabet on your larger piece of cardboard, you can go through all 25 Caesar alphabets quickly, substituting the real-letter equivalents for each letter in your cipher message till you get the right one. Remember to take your cipher letters from the narrow strip, and your real letters from the larger piece of cardboard.

Let's try it.

Here's the St. Cyr machine set for a Caesar alphabet beginning with B:

Now try to decipher the message, using the alphabet shown. You shouldn't have to go farther than the first word to find out if you have the right alphabet or not:

real: K P I X B M Z
cipher: L Q J Y C N A

That doesn't look at all promising—so slide your Caesar strip along letter by letter, deciphering the first word of the message according to each new alphabet, till you find a word that makes sense. Then decipher the rest of the message. (The answer is under B on page 155.)

You can use your St. Cyr machine to test for many other substitution ciphers too. To test for Backwards Alphabet, you can use your regular St. Cyr strip. (Make sure you label each new strip you make.) You can use the Caesar strip for Half-and-Half alphabet—but be careful to remember to stop after M in the top alphabet and after Z in the alphabet on the strip:

You can make St. Cyr strips for number ciphers too:

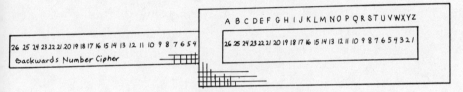

Forwards Number Cipher

Backwards Number Cipher

Of course sooner or later you'll find a cipher the St. Cyr machine won't work for—and then you'll have to go back to the rules. Here's a message in a cipher whose symbols were made up especially for this book:

∨ ⋀∨∿⊙　−⊓+>∨∿　⊓✳　＼　◇∨3

⊔∨✳✳＼⊏∨　•>＼•　⊓✳　•⊐〉⊏>

•⊐　✳⊐﹤⋀∨

The first thing you should notice is that the message doesn't seem to have been divided into fake "words"— which will make deciphering it a lot easier.

The first step is to copy down each *different* symbol used in the message. Be careful you don't just copy down the message—don't write down any symbol more than once. Then, next to each *different* symbol, write down the number of times it appears in the message:

∨ - 7	＼- 3
⋏- 2	◇- 1
∿ - 2	3 - 1
⊙ - 1	⊔ - 1
— - 1	⊏ - 2
⊓ - 3	• - 4
+ - 1	⊐ - 3
> - 3	꒕ - 1
✳ - 5	⟨ - 1

Now put that list aside for the moment and check through the message for:

1. 1-letter words?
   —Yes, there's 1: ＼
2. Double letters?
   —Yes, one set: ✳✳
3. 2-letter words?
   —Yes, 3: ⊓✳ twice, and •⊐ once
4. 3-letter words?
   —Yes: ◇∨3
5. 4-letter words?
   —Yes: •>＼•
6. Pattern words?
   —Yes, 3: ∨⋏∨∿⊙
   and ⊔∨✳✳＼⊏∨
   and •>＼•

Now look at your count again—the list you made of how many times each symbol was used in the message. There's a pretty good candidate for E in the very first symbol on the list. Not only was ∨ used 7 times—more than any of the other letters—but it also begins one word and ends two others. Especially since you know E is the most common last letter of words, it's worth a try!

Copy the message down on a piece of graph paper, and write an E—*in pencil*—above each symbol ∨ in the message:

Some cipher experts use colored pencils instead of regular lead pencils at this stage of deciphering. If you used, say, a red pencil to write down the E's this time, and all the other letters that seemed to work with E, you could use a blue pencil later if you wanted to try another letter for ∨ and see how the other possible letters went with that.

Now how about that 1-letter word? Ignore the possibility of its being an initial, at least for now. The rules tell you that A is much more common than I or O as a 1-letter word—so why not try A? Luckily it appears in more than one word, so you can fill it in in several places:

```
 E     E                   E              A        E
 v  ✗  V  ~  ⊙    -  ⊓  +  >  V  ~    ⊓  ✳    \      ◇  V  3

    E        A  E              A
 ⊔  V  ✳  ✳  \  ⊏  V    ·  >  \  ·    ⊓  ✳    ·  ⊐  彡 ⊏  >

                    E
 ·  ⊐     ✳  ⊐  <  ✗  V
```

Two of the words the symbol \ appears in are pattern words—and one of them begins and ends with the same symbol. Remember that T is common at both the beginnings and ends of words—and that THAT is the most common 4-letter word in English. It certainly fits the pattern of ·>\· . Let's try it:

```
 E     E                   E              A        E
 v  ✗  V  ~  ⊙    -  ⊓  +  >  V  ~    ⊓  ✳    \      ◇  V  3

    E        A  E    T  H  A  T
 ⊔  V  ✳  ✳  \  ⊏  V    ·  >  \  ·    ⊓  ✳    ·  ⊐  彡 ⊏  >

                    E
 ·  ⊐     ✳  ⊐  <  ✗  V
```

Fortunately you can fill in a couple more ·'s and >'s:

```
 E     E                H  E              A        E
 v  ✗  V  ~  ⊙    -  ⊓  +  >  V  ~    ⊓  ✳    \      ◇  V  3

    E        A  E    T  H  A  T              T        H
 ⊔  V  ✳  ✳  \  ⊏  V    ·  >  \  ·    ⊓  ✳    ·  ⊐  彡 ⊏  >

 T                  E
 ·  ⊐     ✳  ⊐  <  ✗  V
```

Now how about the 2-letter words? One of them begins with T, if you're right about the symbol •. TO is on your list of common 2-letter words—so you could try TO for • ⅃ Remember to fill in all the other possible O's:

And now how about the other 2-letter word: ⊓ ✳ , which appears twice? The rules tell you that likely possibilities are OF, IN, IT, and IS. ⊓ ✳ can't be OF if ⅃ is right for O. Looks as if there's a good chance the first letter— ⊓ —is an I, even though it does appear in only one other word. What about the second letter, ✳ ? Your count tells you ✳ appears 5 times, once doubled. It must therefore be a pretty common letter. Your list of common letters shows E, T, A, O, N, R, I, S, H, and D, in that order. T is a common letter, doubled as well as by itself—but you seem to have a T already. You also probably have an E, an A, and an O. Besides if ⊓ , the first letter in this mysterious 2-letter word, is an I, the second letter isn't very likely to be another vowel—the possible "words" then would be IA, IE, IO, or IU. That leaves N, R, S, H, and D. You probably already have an H, so you can forget that. But how can you tell which of the remaining possible letters to use? Remember that ✕ appears doubled as well as by itself. Common double letters, says the frequency table list, are SS, EE, TT, FF, LL, MM, and OO. Of those, the only one we're left with as a possibility for the second letter of a 2-letter word is S—a commonly used letter, both doubled and alone, and one that ends a commonly used 2-letter word: IS. (You see how much guesswork there is in cipher solving. Even the experts do a lot of it!)

Let's try I for ⊓ and S for ✕ , filling them in each time they appear:

E	E			I	HE		I	S	A		E
	E				E	THAT		I	S	T	O	H
T	O	S	O		E						

From now on, the guesswork really takes over. You usually reach that point sooner or later when deciphering a message—the point at which you've filled in just about all the letters you can using the rules, and you have to begin guessing at whole words. It often also helps to try to figure out what the message is trying to communicate—a warning or directions—and its general subject matter. The message we've been working on has nothing to do with pirates, but you know that many of the messages earlier in this book did. If you found yourself earlier in the book with the partially deciphered word

I_ATE

—you could be pretty sure of what it was!

The partially deciphered words in the message we've just been working on are as follows (the completely deciphered words are in parentheses):

E__ E__ __ __I __HE__ (IS A) __E__

__ESSA__E (THAT IS) TO__ __H (TO) SO __ __E

Can you guess at the remaining words? Try especially the word __ ESSA __ E—and if you guess it, don't forget to fill in any other letters that are replaced by ⎵ or ⊏ in the message. If you get that one word, you may be able to figure out the subject matter of the message—and that should help with the words __I__HE__ and SO__ __E.

(The completed message deciphered, along with the alphabet used for enciphering it, is under C on page 155.)

Messages to Solve

In some of the more obvious messages that follow, all you'll have is the message; you'll have to figure out what the code or cipher is. In other messages, there'll be a clue. Remember that most decoding and deciphering takes a long time and a lot of practice—even for experts. So—get yourself some nice sharp pencils, a good eraser, lots of paper and graph paper, and your cipher machines. If one message stumps you, go on to the next. (The answers are in a separate section beginning on page 155.) Don't work so long on one message that you get sick of the whole thing. Good luck—and most of all, enjoy!

1. Up and down, on the fence,
   That's the way that this makes sense!
   DAUAO TEGRI RCLLA HSALC

2. 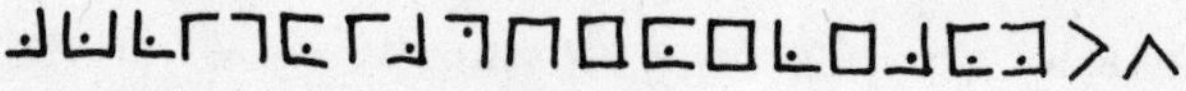

3. EDOC RAW LIVIC NI:
   MEET TRENCHCOAT ON TUESDAY HER
   YOU THE UNDER JAY WITHOUT THE
   RECEIVED WOMAN THE STREET FAIL
   LARGE LAST IN BROKEN AT AND FLAT
   FRIDAY THE STREETLIGHT MIDNIGHT
   GIVE PACKAGE NIGHT

4.

01110	00100	10010	01110
00100	00011	00111	10011
01101	10010	00100	10010
01110	01101	01000	00100
01010	01100	10000	10000
00100	00000	00010	10001
10011	01011	01101	
10001	00100	01011	

5. 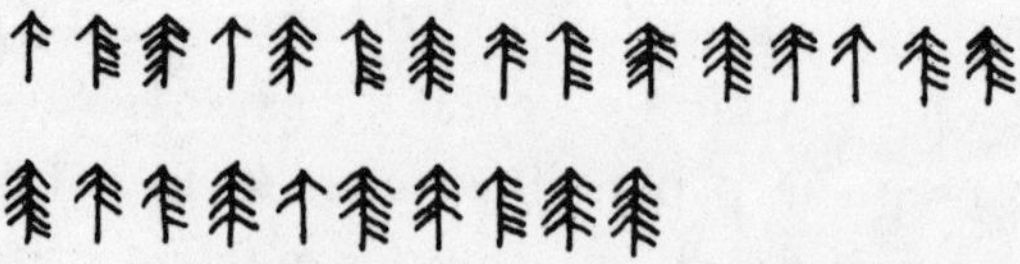

6. EGNAR TSWOH DRAHS IHTRE HPICN ACKOO
   LNEHW TISIY LLAER OSELP MISXY

7.

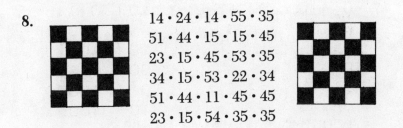

8.

14 · 24 · 14 · 55 · 35
51 · 44 · 15 · 15 · 45
23 · 15 · 45 · 53 · 35
34 · 15 · 53 · 22 · 34
51 · 44 · 11 · 45 · 45
23 · 15 · 54 · 35 · 35

9.

```
              S
              T
              C
      K   E   Y   M
              R
```

GYLIH YVIJM QZMZJ LIQMV
ITFIK VIMCE ZGUTM EVWXK

10.

11. Five across and then nine down
    You'll find the path that goes to town.
    Down one road and up the next,
    Take that pattern as your text.
    Start at the top and to the left,
    And walk the path if you are deft.

    BCUHU TATYA HLMMA LAUTR OTIEO
    ERGWN EGYFE BEFWD HTGAH

12.

EHT DNE
(TPECXE ROF EHT SREWSNA)

Answers for Chapter Nine

A. Backwards Message Cipher:
YOU CAN STAY UP ALL NIGHT SOLVING
A CIPHER   (X was a null)

B. It was enciphered in a Caesar alphabet beginning with J. Deciphered, the message reads:
CHAPTER NINE MESSAGES TO SOLVE
—not a very satisfying message for a spy, but most spies will tell you their work is sometimes pretty routine!

C.

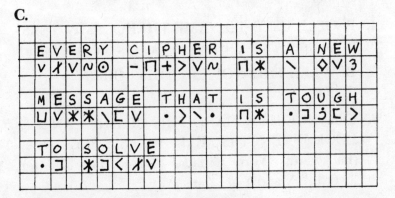

Here's the complete cipher alphabet in case you want to use it:

A B C D E F G H I J K L M
N O P Q R S T U V W X Y Z

1. DRACULA LOATHES GARLIC
(Rail Fence Cipher.)

2. NO PIGS IN THESE PENS
   (Pigpen Cipher. The last three letters—Q, J, and M—
   are nulls.)

3. In Civil War Code:
   MEET THE WOMAN IN THE TRENCHCOAT
   UNDER THE BROKEN STREETLIGHT ON
   JAY STREET AT MIDNIGHT TUESDAY
   WITHOUT FAIL AND GIVE HER THE LARGE
   FLAT PACKAGE YOU RECEIVED LAST
   FRIDAY NIGHT
   (The clue at the beginning is in Backwards Message
   Cipher.)

4. PEOPLE USED TO NAME THEIR COMPUTERS
   (Computer Cipher, based on Bacon's Aabab Cipher)

5. BEWARE THE WOLF IN THIS FOREST
   (Runes)

6. STRANGE HOW HARD THIS CIPHER CAN
   LOOK WHEN IT IS REALLY SO SIMPLE
   (Backwards Word Cipher, divided into 5-letter
   "words." X and Y are nulls.)

7. ELEMENTARY MY DEAR WATSON SAID
   HOLMES
   (Dancing Men Cipher. ⚷ was used for W, as in
   Chapter Seven.)

8. DID YOU SEE THE TWO NEW GNUS AT THE
   ZOO
   (Checkerboard Number Cipher, with X and Z in the
   same square)

9. GO BEFORE DAWN AND BEWARE THE
   CREAKING STAIR
   (St. Cyr Cipher, Key letter: M. Q, P, and C are nulls.)

10. THIS HOUSE IS HAUNTED
    (Hidden Morse—in the roof.)

11. BUT BE CAREFUL OF WHAT YOU MIGHT
    MEET ALONG THE WAY ARGH

    (Twisted Paths. ARGH can be taken as nulls or as part
    of the message, as you wish. The poem gives the pat-
    tern. Note that it is five letters across and nine down.)
    Start at the top and to the left:

Down one road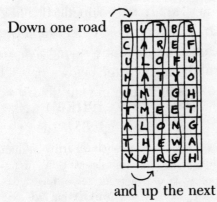

and up the next

12. This is in Ogham:
    TRY MAKING UP SOME OF YOUR OWN NOW

EHT DNE.
YLLAER!

More Books About Codes and Ciphers

There are lots of good books about codes and ciphers—books for people of all ages and all levels of interest. One of the most complete is David Kahn's *The Codebreakers* (New York: The Macmillan Company, 1967)—but since it is more than 1000 pages long, you might want to start with something a little easier! Many encyclopedias have good articles about codes and ciphers (look under *cryptology* or *cryptograms* if you can't find anything under *code* or *cipher*). Then try some of the books listed below—or just look up *codes, ciphers,* and/or *cryptology* in your library's card catalog.

Albert, Burton, Jr. *Codes for Kids.* (Chicago: Albert Whitman and Company, 1976.) Grades 4–6. Contains descriptions of unusual machines and some good ways of disguising secret messages.

Babson, Walt. *All Kinds of Codes.* (New York: Four Winds Press, 1976.) Grade 4 and up. Includes a good chapter about solving ciphers and some tips for using codes to help one's memory!

Epstein, Sam and Beryl. *The First Book of Codes and Ciphers.* (New York: Franklin Watts, Inc., 1956.) Grades 4–6. Includes hobo signs, cattle brands, and how to make and use invisible ink.

Gardner, Martin. *Codes, Ciphers, and Secret Writing.* (New York: Simon & Schuster, Inc., 1972.) Grade 5 and up. Has an interesting chapter about sending messages to outer space, plus information about invisible ink and some fairly advanced ciphers.

James, Elizabeth, and Barkin, Carol. *How to Keep a Secret.* (New York: Lothrop, Lee & Shepard Company, 1978.) Grades 2–6. Includes secret *spoken* languages and tips on hiding messages.

Kohn, Bernice. *Secret Codes and Ciphers.* (New York: Prentice-Hall, Inc., 1968.) Grades 3–7. Includes frequency tables and a short history of 20th-century ciphers.

Laffin, John. *Codes and Ciphers.* (New York: Abelard-Schuman, 1964.) Grade 7 and up. Good for historical background as well as for codes and ciphers themselves.

Lamb, Geoffrey. *Secret Writing Tricks.* (New York: Thomas Nelson & Sons, 1975.) Grade 5 and up. Includes material on how to use key letters and key words, plus a cipher using colors and tips on solving ciphers.

Moore, Dan Tyler, and Warner, Martha. *Cloak and Cipher.* (New York: The Bobbs-Merrill Company, 1962.) Adult. This one is hard, but it offers very good deciphering tips—has very detailed frequency tables. It also contains a lot of information about how codes and ciphers have been used in wartime.

Rothman, Joel, and Tremain, Ruthven. *Secrets with Ciphers and Codes.* (New York: The Macmillan Company, 1969.) Grades 4–6. Concentrates on clever substitution ciphers using shapes.

Sarnoff, Jane, and Ruffins, Reynold. *The Code and Cipher Book.* (New York: Charles Scribner's Sons, 1975.) Grades 1–5. This one is easy to follow, fun to read, and jam-packed with fascinating historical sidelights.

Yerian, Cameron and Margaret, eds. *Codes and Mystery Messages.* (Chicago: Children's Press, 1975.) Grades 1–6. Includes invisible ink, hiding places, games, sign language, and Braille.

Glossary

Cipher: A kind of secret writing in which letters, numbers, or drawings stand for the *letters* of the real alphabet.

Cipher Alphabet: The letters, numbers, or drawings used to stand for the letters of the real alphabet.

Cipher (or *Code*) *Machine:* Any mechanical object used for writing or solving ciphers or codes.

Code: A kind of secret writing in which words, phrases, numbers, or drawings stand for *words* or *phrases* of the real message.

Decipher: To take out of cipher; to solve a cipher.

Decode: To take out of code; to solve a code.

Encipher: To put into cipher; to write a cipher.

Encode: To put into code; to write a code.

Nomenclator: A kind of secret writing combining both cipher and code.

Real Alphabet: A–Z, in the usual order.

Real Message: A secret message before it has been enciphered and/or encoded.

Substitution Cipher: A cipher in which other letters, or numbers or drawings, stand for the letters of the real alphabet. The most common codes, in which words, phrases, etc. stand for the words or phrases in a real message, could be called substitution codes.

Symbol: Something that stands for something else. Symbols are used in codes and ciphers to stand for the words, phrases, or letters of the real message.

Transposition Cipher: A cipher in which the letters used in the real message remain the same but are scrambled. A code in which the words of the real message are scrambled could be called a transposition code.

Index

About the Author

Former teacher and editor, Nancy Garden is the author of *Vampires, Witches, Devils and Demons* and *Berlin: City Split in Two*. She lives in Carlisle, Massachusetts.